EVOLUTION

EVOLUTION

13 wearable hand knits inspired by
The Vintage Shetland Project

Susan Crawford

Susan Crawford Vintage
www.susancrawfordvintage.com

Author / Pattern Writer
Susan Crawford

Creative Director
Susan Crawford

Photography
Charlie Moon

Book Design
Gavin Crawford & Susan Crawford

Technical Editing / Proof Reading
Karen Butler

Editor
Susan Crawford

Publisher
Susan Crawford Vintage

British Library Cataloguing-in-Publication Data
A catalogue record for this book is available from
the British Library
ISBN 978-0-9572286-4-1

Produced on RISC OS on ARMX6 computer system,
using Ovation Pro desktop publishing system, ArtWorks.
All charts created using
The Fair Isle Visualiser charting software by Gavin Crawford.
Typeset using the font families of LondonA and Straight from
The Electronic Font Foundry.

Written, designed and originated in the UK

Contents

Foreword

When I launched the first design in the Evolution collection back in January (2020) I was blissfully unaware of what was in store for us all only a couple of months later. As a result this collection straddles a year when the whole world has been turned on its head, many lives have sadly been lost and many more of us have spent many months separated from friends and family. A collection which was planned to take up just a few months fanned out across the year as demands on my time increased due to the 'lockdown' measures introduced in Britain and necessary isolation due to my ongoing health issues impacted on my life.

My own evolution and that of this collection are very different to what I anticipated, and yet, I hope you'll agree, as you follow me from the beginning of the year to now, that something positive has emerged from this extended journey – both creatively and personally. This project has been uplifting, stimulating, challenging and liberating and I thank you for joining me.

Susan, October 2020

···· EVOLUTION ····

Introduction

Evolution follows nine months in my life as I take design inspiration from The Vintage Shetland Project and create highly wearable, contemporary pieces, each new design evolving from a lace pattern, a clever construction method, a colourwork motif, or even a steek chart, into something completely new; and shows how easily these vintage inspired pieces fit into an everyday wardrobe. With contemporary shaping came the opportunity to offer a much wider sizing range, with every garment pattern covering sizes from 71-157cm (28-62in).

During the ten years I studied the garments found in the Shetland Museum archive I had to be very disciplined, not allowing myself free creative rein, instead focussing on the recreations of these glorious knitted artefacts and delving into their stories. So this latest project, Evolution, has been an absolute joy, allowing me to focus on creativity and wearability. Each design is genuinely now part of my wardrobe. Orchid and Orchidaceae have been worn repeatedly and now the book is complete, I intend to knit additional versions of both in a variety of colours. The Denby slouchy hat has quickly become my go-to hat. Comfy and warm enough to wear round the fields but stylish enough to wear when trying to look tidy! Floribunda and Rosa have each become firm favourites. I would probably wear one or other of these two every single day if I could. I hope to knit the Umbel shawl in several different shades when time allows. It is warm yet light, enveloping but not overwhelming. And so it goes on. As each new piece has been completed, it quickly becomes indispensable.

But more than a knitting pattern collection, Evolution, is also about my own journey over the last nine months as I explored my body's evolution after my double mastectomy and also, after turning fifty. Despite feeling intensely uncomfortable, I was determined that I should be the model for the collection, showing that a 'strangely shaped', fifty year old woman with greying hair, can present clothes in an appealing way and can be visible. Even more so, I wanted to model without the use of prosthesis. I have waited for over two years for delayed reconstructive surgery and do not wear prosthesis on a day to day basis for a number of reasons and I wanted to show that its ok not to do so. There are tens of thousands of women who do not receive reconstructive surgery after breast cancer – for some this is a choice, for some surgery is not an option but for many others, it is very difficult to get access to the surgery. When I began Evolution I was angry, tired and felt helpless, in a constant state of suspense hoping that I would at some point reach the top of the waiting list and get to have the surgery I desperately wanted and needed. As the year has progressed and the world appears to have slipped off its axis along the way, that surgery has become less and less likely and yet, because of this project I have become more and more accepting of who I have become and am still becoming. The person on the front cover of the book photographed at the dawn of the year is very different to the person on the back cover, someone finally becoming happy in her own skin.

Thank you for sharing this journey with me and I do hope that you enjoy knitting the pieces from Evolution as much as I enjoyed creating them.

Abbreviations

approx	–	approximately
BOR	–	beginning of round
cdd	–	centred double decrease; slip 2 together knitwise, knit 1, pass 2 slipped stitches over
cm	–	centimetres
dec	–	decrease
DPNs	–	double pointed needles
g	–	grams
in	–	inches
inc	–	increase
k	–	knit
k1A	–	knit 1 stitch using yarn A
k1tbl	–	knit 1 through back of loop
k2tog	–	knit 2 together
k2togA(B)	–	knit 2 together using yarn A or B as stated
k3tog	–	knit 3 together
kfb	–	knit into front and back of next stitch
m	–	metres
m1	–	make 1, by knitting into back of loop lying between stitches
m1f	–	make 1, by knitting into front of loop lying between stitches
mm	–	millimetres
p	–	purl
p1A(B/D)	–	purl 1 stitch using yarn as stated
p1tbl	–	purl 1 through back of loop
p2tog	–	purl 2 together
patt	–	pattern
pm	–	place marker
rep	–	repeat
RH	–	right hand
RS	–	right side
sk2p	–	slip 1 knitwise, knit 2 together, pass slip stitch over
skp	–	slip 1 knitwise, knit 1, pass slip stitch over
sl1	–	slip 1 st (purlwise unless directed otherwise)
sm	–	slip marker
st(s)	–	stitch(es)
w&t	–	wrap and turn – **RS rows** slip st to right hand needle, bring yarn forward, slip st back to left hand needle, take yarn back, turn; **WS rows** slip st to right hand needle, take yarn back, slip st back to left hand needle, bring yarn forward, turn
WS	–	wrong side
yds	–	yards
yo	–	yarn over (also known as yarn forward or yarn round needle)

Gallery

Orchid page 75

···· EVOLUTION ····

Denby page 91

Floribunda page 99

···· EVOLUTION ····

Gallica page 107

···· EVOLUTION ····

Umbel page 115

···· EVOLUTION ····

Lanatus page 127

···· EVOLUTION ····

···· EVOLUTION ····

···· EVOLUTION ····

Cloudin page 137

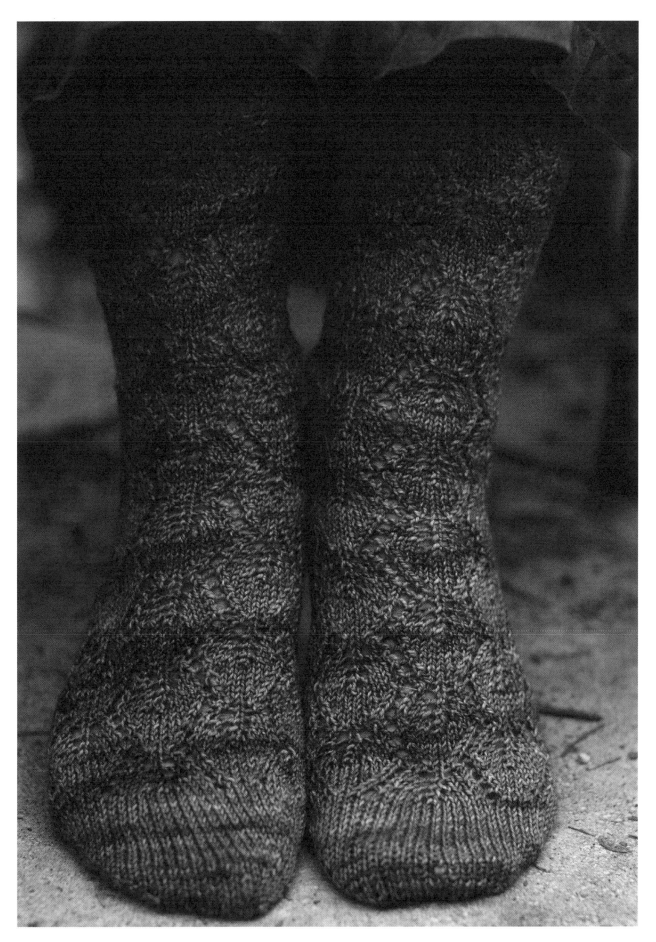

···· EVOLUTION ····

Rosa page 145

Steek page 153

· · · · EVOLUTION · · · ·

···· EVOLUTION ····

Tavis page 159

Annemor page 165

···· EVOLUTION ····

···· E V O L U T I O N ····

Maggy page 175

Patterns

Orchid

Orchid was the first design created for Evolution and was inspired by the lacy yoke on Dorothy from The Vintage Shetland Project.

Orchid is an easy-to-wear, comfortable sweater featuring a beautiful lace yoke. The sweater is worked in the round from the bottom up, on reaching the armholes the body is put to one side, then the sleeves are knitted, then the body and sleeves are joined together and worked in one piece, in the round. Short row shaping is worked on the upper back section of the body ensuring the front neckline doesn't sit too high. Once the short rows are completed the lace yoke is then worked. This simple, 12 stitch lace pattern creates a striking orchid petal outline.

The body is unshaped, its finished length designed to sit roughly on the hip bone; however it can simply be knitted shorter or longer depending on the finished length preferred. To shorten the upper body, fewer rounds can be worked before commencing the lace yoke, avoiding any complicated changes. Both charts and written instructions are provided for the lace section, with the chart being read from right to left on every round.

The Orchid sample shown is knitted in Excelana 4 Ply, a standard fingering weight pure wool, using a blend of British breed fleeces from the Exmoor Mule and Bluefaced Leicester sheep, to create a soft, yet sturdy, yarn in the beautiful shade of Coral Lombard.

Orchid is designed to be worn with approximately 15–20cm (6–8in) of positive ease.

Orchid

YARN
Susan Crawford Excelana 4 Ply, 100% British wool (159m / 174yds per 50g skein)
5 (6, 7, 7, 8, 9, 10, 10, 11) skeins, shade Carol Lombard
Yarn kits available from susancrawfordvintage.com

GAUGE
25 sts and 32 rounds = 10cm (4in) measured over stocking stitch, worked in the round.
We obtained this gauge using 3.5mm needles.

If necessary use an alternative needle size to obtain the correct gauge.

SUGGESTED NEEDLES
Small needles: 3.25mm (US 3) circular needle (40–60cm in length)
                    3.25mm (US 3) circular needle (80–100cm in length)
                    Set of 3.25mm (US 3) DPNs

Large needles: 3.5mm (US 4) circular needle (40cm in length)
                    3.5mm (US 4) circular needle (80–100cm in length)
                    Set of 3.5mm (US 4) DPNs

NOTIONS
Waste yarn or stitch holders
Stitch markers

SAMPLE SHOWN
Orchid is modelled by Susan who is wearing the 4th size with 15cm (6in) of ease.

SIZING AND FINISHING GUIDE

Choose the 'To fit' size closest to your actual chest measurement when deciding which size to knit, bearing in mind the fit you would like to achieve. Use in conjunction with the Schematic to identify which size you should knit.

The measurements given represent the dimensions of the knitting after finishing and blocking according to the pattern instructions and will help you identify which size you should knit. They can also be used to help make adjustments to the finished size of your knitting if needed. The Schematic and the measurements should be used to assist in the pinning-out process to ensure the finished piece is the correct size. Measurements are given in centimetres with inches shown in parentheses.

		1st Size	2nd Size	3rd Size	4th Size	5th Size	6th Size	7th Size	8th Size	9th Size
To fit chest		71–76 (28–30)	81–86 (32–34)	91–97 (36–38)	102–107 (40–42)	112–117 (44–46)	122–127 (48–50)	132–137 (52–54)	142–147 (56–58)	152–157 (60–62)
Finished Measurements										
a	Chest circumference	90½ (36¼)	101 (40½)	111 (44½)	120 (48)	131 (52½)	141½ (56½)	153 (61¼)	162½ (65)	172 (68¾)
b	Length to underarm	25 (10)	26 (10½)	26 (10½)	27 (10¾)	28 (11¼)	28 (11¼)	29 (11½)	29 (11½)	30 (12)
c	Yoke depth	19½ (7¾)	20½ (8¼)	22 (8¾)	23 (9¼)	25 (10)	27 (10¾)	28 (11¼)	29 (11½)	31½ (12½)
d	Length	44½ (17¾)	46½ (18½)	48 (19¼)	50 (20)	53 (21¼)	55 (22)	57 (22¾)	58 (23¼)	61½ (24½)
h	Sleeve length	43 (17¼)	43 (17¼)	44 (17½)	44 (17½)	45 (18)	45 (18)	46 (18½)	46 (18½)	47 (19)
m	Upper arm circumference	29½ (11¾)	32½ (13)	35 (14)	37 (14¾)	40½ (16¼)	43 (17¼)	47 (18¾)	49½ (19¾)	53 (21¼)

SCHEMATIC

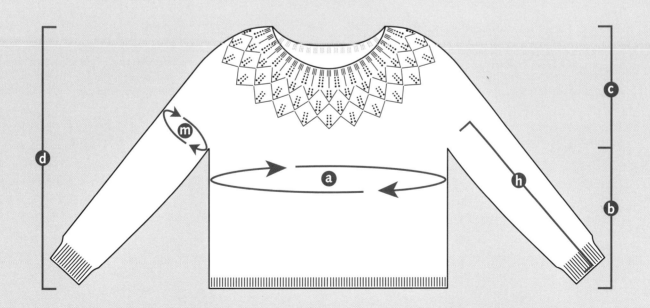

DIRECTIONS

BODY

Using smaller circular needle (80–100cm), cast on 224 (252, 276, 300, 328, 352, 380, 404, 428) sts using long tail cast-on method. Join into a round taking care not to twist sts, placing a marker to indicate beginning of round.

Welt

Next round: * K2, p2; rep from * to end of round.
Repeat this round until ribbing measures approximately 2½cm (1in) from cast-on edge, increasing 2 (0, 2, 0, 0, 2, 2, 2, 2) sts evenly across last round; 226 (252, 278, 300, 328, 354, 382, 406, 430) sts.

Lower Body

Change to larger circular needle (80–100cm).
Commence working in stocking stitch (knit every round).
Continue as set until work measures 25 (26, 26, 27, 28, 28, 29, 29, 30) cm, (10, 10½, 10½, 10¾, 11¼, 11¼, 11½, 11½, 12 in) from cast-on edge and placing marker after 113 (126, 139, 150, 164, 177, 191, 203, 215) sts to indicate side seam a few rounds before this measurement is reached.

Armhole Divide

Next round: * K to 4 (5, 5, 6, 6, 7, 7, 8, 8) sts beyond marker, place last 8 (10, 10, 12, 12, 14, 14, 16, 16) sts worked onto waste yarn, removing marker; rep from * once more; 16 (20, 20, 24, 24, 28, 28, 32, 32) sts dec, 210 (232, 258, 276, 304, 326, 354, 374, 398) sts.
Your sts will now be divided as follows: 105 (116, 129, 138, 152, 163, 177, 187, 199) sts for front, 105 (116, 129, 138, 152, 163, 177, 187, 199) sts for back.

SLEEVES

Using smaller DPNs, cast on 48 (52, 52, 56, 56, 60, 60, 64, 68) sts using long tail cast-on method. Join into a round taking care not to twist sts, placing a marker to indicate beginning of round.
Next round: * K2, p2; rep from * to end of round.
Repeat this round until cuff measures approximately 5cm (2in) from cast-on edge, increasing 0 (1, 1, 0, 1, 0, 1, 0, 0) st at beginning of last round; 48 (53, 53, 56, 57, 60, 61, 64, 68) sts.

Change to larger DPNs.
Next round (Inc): K1, m1, k to 1 st before marker, m1, k1; 2 sts inc.
K 7 (5, 5, 5, 3, 3, 1, 1, 1) rounds.
Next round (Inc): K1, m1, k to 1 st before marker, m1, k1; 2 sts inc.

Repeat last 8 (6, 6, 6, 4, 4, 2, 2, 2) rounds a further 7 (0, 10, 14, 9, 16, 1, 5, 7) times, changing to larger circular needle (40cm) when stitch count allows if preferred; 66 (57, 77, 88, 79, 96, 67, 78, 86) sts.

K 9 (7, 7, 7, 5, 5, 3, 3, 3) rounds.
Next round (Inc): K1, m1, k to 1 st before marker, m1, k1; 2 sts inc.

Repeat last 10 (8, 8, 8, 6, 6, 4, 4, 4) rounds a further 3 (11, 4, 1, 10, 5, 24, 22, 22) times; 74 (81, 87, 92, 101, 108, 117, 124, 132) sts.

Work without further shaping until sleeve measures 43 (43, 44, 44, 45, 45, 46, 46, 47) cm (17¼, 17¼, 17½, 17½, 18, 18, 18½, 18½, 19 in) from cast-on edge.

Armhole Divide

Without working, move sts around on needles, placing last 4 (5, 5, 6, 6, 7, 7, 8, 8) sts before marker and first 4 (5, 5, 6, 6, 7, 7, 8, 8) sts after marker onto waste yarn, removing marker. Break yarn; 66 (71, 77, 80, 89, 94, 103, 108, 116) sts.

JOIN YOKE

Using larger circular needle (80–100cm), and with RS facing, k across 105 (116, 129, 138, 152, 163, 177, 187, 199) sts on back, then k across 66 (71, 77, 80, 89, 94, 103, 108, 116) sts on first sleeve, pm (left front), k across 105 (116, 129, 138, 152, 163, 177, 187, 199) sts on front, pm (right front), then k across 66 (71, 77, 80, 89, 94, 103, 108, 116) sts on second sleeve; 342 (374, 412, 436, 482, 514, 560, 590, 630) sts.

Next round (Partial): K across 52 (58, 64, 69, 76, 81, 88, 93, 99) sts of back, pm for end of round. Round now begins at centre back.

Work 10 (10, 12, 12, 14, 14, 16, 17, 18) rounds straight.

You will now work a series of decreases before moving on to a section of short rows and then following the chart. Read each decrease round and circle instructions for your size before proceeding.

1st, 2nd, 3rd, 5th and 7th sizes only
Next round (Dec): K 2 (10, 9, 9, 0), * k2tog, k 8 (6, 6, 9, 8);
rep from * to last 0 (4, 3, 0, 0) sts, k 0 (4, 3, 0, 0).

4th, 6th, 8th, and 9th sizes only
Next round (Dec): K 4 (4, 5, 4), [k2tog, k 9 (9, 11, 10)]
4 (2, 19, 18) times, [k2tog, k 10 (8, 10, 9)] 29 (46, 7, 17)
times, [k2tog, k 9 (9, 11, 10)] 3 (2, 19, 18) times, k2tog,
k 5 (4, 5, 5).

All sizes
34 (45, 50, 37, 43, 51, 56, 46, 54) sts dec, 308 (329, 362,
399, 439, 463, 504, 544, 576) sts.

Work 5 (8, 9, 8, 10, 14, 14, 11, 14) rounds straight.

1st, 2nd, 3rd, 5th and 7th sizes only
Next round (Dec): K 2 (10, 12, 9, 0), * k2tog, k 7 (5, 5, 8,
7); rep from * to last 0 (4, 7, 0, 0) sts, k 0 (4, 7, 0, 0).

4th, 6th, 8th, and 9th sizes only
Next round (Dec): K 4 (4, 5, 4), [k2tog, k 8 (8, 10, 9)] 4 (2,
19, 18) times, [k2tog, k 9 (7, 9, 8)] 29 (46, 7, 17) times,
[k2tog, k 8 (8, 10, 9)] 3 (2, 19, 18) times, k2tog, k 4 (3,
4, 4).

All sizes
34 (45, 49, 37, 43, 51, 56, 46, 54) sts dec, 274 (284, 313,
362, 396, 412, 448, 498, 522) sts.

Work 2 (3, 4, 5, 7, 8, 9, 9, 9) rounds straight.

1st, 3rd, 5th, 6th and 7th sizes only
Next round (Dec): K 2 (12, 12, 9, 0), * k2tog, k 6 (4, 7, 6,
6); rep from * to last 0 (7, 6, 3, 0) sts, k 0 (7, 6, 3, 0).

2nd, 4th, 8th and 9th sizes only
Next round (Dec): K 2 (4, 4, 4), [k2tog, k 5 (7, 9, 8)] 10 (4,
19, 18) times, [k2tog, k 4 (8, 8, 7)] 23 (29, 7, 17) times,
[k2tog, k 5 (7, 9, 8)] 10 (3, 19, 18) times, k2tog, k 2 (3,
4, 3).

All sizes
34 (44, 49, 37, 42, 50, 56, 46, 54) sts dec, 240 (240, 264,
325, 354, 362, 392, 452, 468) sts.

4th, 5th, 6th, 7th, 8th and 9th sizes only
Work 3 (3, 4, 5, 5, 7) rounds straight.

5th, 6th and 7th sizes only
Next round (Dec): K 12 (9, 0), * k2tog, k 6 (5, 5); rep from
* to last 6 (3, 0) sts, k 6 (3, 0); 42 (50, 56) sts dec, 312
(312, 336) sts.

4th, 8th and 9th sizes only
Next round (Dec): K 3 (4, 3), [k2tog, k 6 (8, 7)] 4 (19, 18)
times, [k2tog, k 7 (7, 6)] 29 (7, 17) times, [k2tog, k 6 (8, 7)]
3 (19, 18) times, k2tog, k3; 37 (46, 54) sts dec, 288 (406,
414) sts.

8th and 9th sizes only
Work 4 (5) rounds straight.

Next round (Dec): K3, [k2tog, k7 (6)] 19 (18) times, [k2tog,
k 6 (5)] 7 (17) times, [k2tog, k 7 (6)] 19 (18) times, k2tog, k
3 (2); 46 (54) sts dec, 360 (360) sts.

All sizes
240 (240, 264, 288, 312, 312, 336, 360, 360) sts.
Work 1 round straight.

Short Row Section
Next row (RS): K to 9 sts after left front marker, w&t.
Next row (WS): P to 9 sts after right front marker, w&t.
Next row: K to 7 (7, 7, 7, 8, 8, 9, 9, 10) sts before last turn,
w&t.
Next row: P to 7 (7, 7, 7, 8, 8, 9, 9, 10) sts before last turn,
w&t.
Repeat last 2 rows twice more, knitting back to beginning of
round marker after last turn.
Next round: K to end, reconciling w&ts and removing
additional markers as you work – leaving beginning of
round marker in place.

Place Yoke Chart
This section is worked in the round. Use either the chart or
written instructions provided.
Commencing with line 1 of Yoke Chart, work 12 st patt rep
20 (20, 22, 24, 26, 26, 28, 30, 30) times across round.
Continue in this manner until all 39 lines of chart have been
completed.
You will work decreases on line 21 to give 200 (200, 220,
240, 260, 260, 280, 300, 300) sts, on line 29 to give
160 (160, 176, 192, 208, 208, 224, 240, 240) sts and finally
on line 39 to give 120 (120, 132, 144, 156, 156, 168, 180,
180) sts.
Yoke Chart is now complete.

Neckband

Change to smaller circular needle (40–60cm).

Next round: * K2, p2; rep from * to end of round.

Repeat this round until neckband measures approximately 2cm (¾in) from cast-on edge

Cast off in rib.

FINISHING

Graft together the 2 sets of 8 (10, 10, 12, 12, 14, 14, 16, 16) sts held on waste yarn at each underarm.

Soak in lukewarm soapy water, rinse if required, then pin out to size and leave to dry flat.

Darn in any ends.

WRITTEN INSTRUCTIONS FOR CHART

YOKE CHART

Round 1: K1, yo, skp, k7, k2tog, yo.

Round 2 and all even-numbered rounds except round 18: Knit.

Round 3: K1, yo, k1, skp, k5, k2tog, k1, yo.

Round 5: K1, yo, k2, skp, k3, k2tog, k2, yo.

Round 7: K1, yo, k3, skp, k1, k2tog, k3, yo.

Round 9: K1, yo, k4, sk2p, k4, yo.

Round 11: K4, k2tog, yo, k1, yo, skp, k3.

Round 13: K3, k2tog, (k1, yo) twice, k1, skp, k2.

Round 15: K2, k2tog, k2, yo, k1, yo, k2, skp, k1.

Round 17: K1, k2tog, k3, yo, k1, yo, k3, skp.

Round 18: Knit to within last st of round, pm for new BOR.

Round 19: Removing previous BOR marker at start of round, sk2p, k4, yo, k1, yo, k4.

Round 21 (Dec): K1, skp, k7, k2tog.

Round 23: K1, yo, skp, k5, k2tog, yo.

Round 25: K1, yo, k1, skp, k3, k2tog, k1, yo.

Round 27: K1, yo, k2, skp, k1, k2tog, k2, yo.

Round 29 (Dec): K4, sk2p, k3.

Round 31: K2, k2tog, yo, k1, yo, skp, k1.

Round 33: K1, k2tog, (k1, yo) twice, k1, skp.

Round 35: K1, k2tog, (k1, yo) twice, k1, skp.

Round 37: K1, k2tog, (k1, yo) twice, k1, skp.

Round 39 (Dec): K1, k2tog, k3, skp.

CHART NOTES

This lace pattern has a decrease which uses a stitch from the previous round in order to align the patterning correctly.

Round 18: Follow chart as set to last stitch.

Round 19: Work first sk2p using the un-worked stitch from previous round, then continue following chart as set.

Ensure the end of round marker is positioned immediately before the decrease.

Yoke Chart

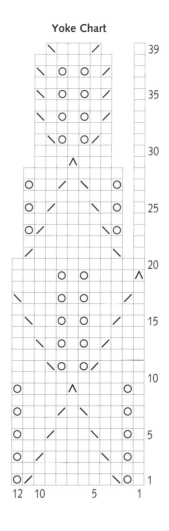

Key

☐	knit
╱	k2tog
╲	skp
O	yo
Λ	sk2p

Orchidaceae

Orchidaceae is a DK weight version of Orchid and was also inspired by the lace yoke of Dorothy from The Vintage Shetland Project. I enjoyed wearing Orchid so much I couldn't resist also creating a slightly heavier-weight version that is knitted on larger needles and knits up quickly with striking results.

Orchidacea is an easy-to-wear, comfortable sweater featuring a beautiful lace yoke. The sweater is worked in the round from the bottom up, on reaching the armholes the body is put to one side, then the sleeves are knitted, then the body and sleeves are joined together and worked in one piece, in the round. Short row shaping is worked on the upper back section of the body ensuring the front neckline doesn't sit too high. Once the short rows are completed the lace yoke is then worked. This simple, 12 stitch lace pattern creates a striking orchid petal outline.

The body is unshaped, its finished length designed to sit roughly on the hip bone; however it can simply be knitted shorter or longer depending on the finished length preferred. To shorten the upper body, fewer rounds can be worked before commencing the lace yoke, avoiding any complicated changes. Both charts and written instructions are provided for the lace section, with the chart being read from right to left on every round.

The Orchid sample shown is knitted in Excelana DK, a standard DK weight pure wool blend, using a blend of British breed fleeces from the Exmoor Mule and Bluefaced Leicester sheep, to create a soft, plump yarn. I knitted the sample using Cinnamon, a warm but pale terracotta shade.

Orchid is designed to be worn with approximately 15–20cm (6–8in) of positive ease, but for a more fitted look as shown in the photographs, choose a size with a finished chest measurement only approximately 5cm (2in) greater than your chest measurement.

Orchidaceae

YARN

Susan Crawford Excelana DK, 100% British wool (247m / 270yds per 100g skein)

4 (4, 5, 5, 6, 6, 7, 7, 8) skeins, shade Cinnamon

Yarn kits available from susancrawfordvintage.com

GAUGE

22 sts and 30 rounds = 10cm (4in) measured over stocking stitch, worked in the round.

We obtained this gauge using 4mm needles.

If necessary use an alternative needle size to obtain the correct gauge.

SUGGESTED NEEDLES

Small needles: 3.25mm (US 3) circular needle (40–60cm in length)

                     3.25mm (US 3) circular needle (80–100cm in length)

                     Set of 3.25mm (US 3) DPNs

Large needles: 4mm (US 6) circular needle (40cm in length)

                     4mm (US 6) circular needle (80–100cm in length)

                     Set of 4mm (US 6) DPNs

NOTIONS

Waste yarn or stitch holders

Stitch markers

SAMPLE SHOWN

Orchidaceae is modelled by Susan who is wearing the 3rd size with 7cm (2¾in) of ease for a more fitted look than suggested.

SIZING AND FINISHING GUIDE

Choose the 'To fit' size closest to your actual chest measurement when deciding which size to knit, bearing in mind the fit you would like to achieve. Use in conjunction with the Schematic to identify which size you should knit.

The measurements given represent the dimensions of the knitting after finishing and blocking according to the pattern instructions and will help you identify which size you should knit. They can also be used to help make adjustments to the finished size of your knitting if needed. The Schematic and the measurements should be used to assist in the pinning-out process to ensure the finished piece is the correct size. Measurements are given in centimetres with inches shown in parentheses.

		1st Size	2nd Size	3rd Size	4th Size	5th Size	6th Size	7th Size	8th Size	9th Size
To fit chest		71–76 (28–30)	81–86 (32–34)	91–97 (36–38)	102–107 (40–42)	112–117 (44–46)	122–127 (48–50)	132–137 (52–54)	142–147 (56–58)	152–157 (60–62)
Finished Measurements										
a	Chest circumference	92 (36¾)	102 (40¾)	112 (44¾)	122 (48¾)	132 (52¾)	142 (56¾)	153 (61)	163 (65)	173 (69)
b	Length to underarm	25 (10)	26 (10½)	26 (10½)	27 (10¾)	28 (11¼)	28 (11¼)	29 (11½)	29 (11½)	30 (12)
c	Yoke depth	20 (8)	21 (8½)	22 (8¾)	23½ (9½)	25 (10)	27 (10¾)	28½ (11¼)	29½ (11¾)	31½ (12½)
d	Length	45 (18)	47 (19)	48 (19¼)	50½ (20¼)	53 (21¼)	55 (22)	57½ (23)	58½ (23¼)	61½ (24½)
h	Sleeve length	43 (17¼)	43 (17¼)	44 (17½)	44 (17½)	45 (18)	45 (18)	46 (18½)	46 (18½)	47 (19)
m	Upper arm circumference	29½ (11¾)	32½ (13)	35 (14)	37½ (15)	40½ (16¼)	43 (17¼)	46½ (18½)	49½ (19¾)	52½ (21)

SCHEMATIC

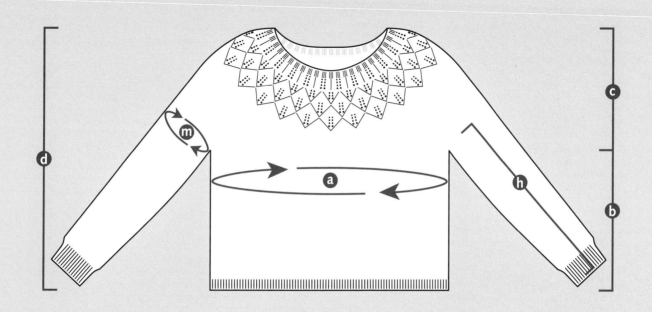

DIRECTIONS

BODY

Using smaller circular needle (80–100cm), cast on 200 (224, 244, 268, 288, 312, 336, 356, 380) sts using long tail cast-on method. Join into a round taking care not to twist sts, placing a marker to indicate beginning of round.

Welt

Next round: * K2, p2; rep from * to end of round.
Repeat this round until ribbing measures approximately 2½cm (1in) from cast-on edge, increasing 2 (0, 2, 0, 2, 0, 0, 2, 0) sts evenly across last round; 202 (224, 246, 268, 290, 312, 336, 358, 380) sts.

Lower Body

Change to larger circular needle (80–100cm).
Commence working in stocking stitch (knit every round).
Continue as set until work measures 25 (26, 26, 27, 28, 28, 29, 29, 30) cm, (10, 10½, 10½, 10¾, 11¼, 11¼, 11½, 11½, 12 in) from cast-on edge and placing marker after 101 (112, 123, 134, 145, 156, 168, 179, 190) sts to indicate side seam a few rounds before this measurement is reached.

Armhole Divide

Next round: * K to 3 (4, 4, 5, 5, 6, 6, 7, 7) sts beyond marker, place last 6 (8, 8, 10, 10, 12, 12, 14, 14) sts worked onto waste yarn, removing marker; rep from * once more; 12 (16, 16, 20, 20, 24, 24, 28, 28) sts dec, 190 (208, 230, 248, 270, 288, 312, 330, 352) sts.
Your sts will now be divided as follows:
95 (104, 115, 124, 135, 144, 156, 165, 176) sts for front, 95 (104, 115, 124, 135, 144, 156, 165, 176) sts for back.

SLEEVES

Using smaller DPNs, cast on 44 (44, 48, 48, 52, 52, 56, 56, 60) sts using long tail cast-on method. Join into a round taking care not to twist sts, placing a marker to indicate beginning of round.
Next round: * K2, p2; rep from * to end of round.
Repeat this round until cuff measures approximately 5cm (2in) from cast-on edge, increasing 1 (1, 1, 0, 1, 1, 0, 1, 1) st at beginning of last round; 45 (45, 49, 48, 53, 53, 56, 57, 61) sts.

Change to larger DPNs.
Next round (Inc): K1, m1, k to 1 st before marker, m1, k1; 2 sts inc.
K9 (5, 5, 3, 3, 3, 3, 1, 1) rounds.
Next round (Inc): K1, m1, k to 1 st before marker, m1, k1; 2 sts inc.

Repeat last 10 (6, 6, 4, 4, 4, 4, 2, 2) rounds a further 4 (0, 3, 0, 2, 10, 15, 0, 0) times, changing to circular needle (40cm) when stitch count allows if preferred; 57 (49, 59, 52, 61, 77, 90, 61, 65) sts.

K11 (7, 7, 5, 5, 5, 5, 3, 3) rounds.
Next round (Inc): K1, m1, k to 1 st before marker, m1, k1; 2 sts inc.

Repeat last 12 (8, 8, 6, 6, 6, 6, 4, 4) rounds a further 3 (10, 8, 14, 13, 8, 5, 23, 24) times; 65 (71, 77, 82, 89, 95, 102, 109, 115) sts.

Work without further shaping until sleeve measures 43 (43, 44, 44, 45, 45, 46, 46, 47) cm (17¼, 17¼, 17½, 17½, 18, 18, 18½, 18½, 19 in) from cast-on edge.

Armhole Divide

Without working, move sts around on needles, placing last 3 (4, 4, 5, 5, 6, 6, 7, 7) sts before marker and first 3 (4, 4, 5, 5, 6, 6, 7, 7) sts after marker onto waste yarn, removing marker. Break yarn; 59 (63, 69, 72, 79, 83, 90, 95, 101) sts.

JOIN YOKE

Using larger circular needle (80–100cm), and with RS facing, k across 95 (104, 115, 124, 135, 144, 156, 165, 176) sts on back, then k across 59 (63, 69, 72, 79, 83, 90, 95, 101) sts on first sleeve, pm (left front), k across 95 (104, 115, 124, 135, 144, 156, 165, 176) sts on front, pm (right front), then k across 59 (63, 69, 72, 79, 83, 90, 95, 101) sts on second sleeve; 308 (334, 368, 392, 428, 454, 492, 520, 554) sts.

Next round (Partial): K across 47 (52, 57, 62, 67, 72, 78, 82, 88) sts of back, pm for end of round. Round now begins at centre back.

Work 8 (10, 12, 14, 16, 18, 18, 20, 24) rounds straight.

You will now work three sets of decreases before moving on to a section of short rows and then following the chart. Read each decrease round and circle instructions for your size before proceeding.

1st size only
Next round (Dec): K4, k2tog, k7, * k2tog, k8; rep from * to last 5 sts, k2tog, k3.

2nd and 3rd sizes only
Next round (Dec): K3, (k2tog, k7) 7 (12) times, (k2tog, k6) 25 (18) times, (k2tog, k7) 7 (12) times, k2tog, k3.

4th and 5th sizes only
Next round (Dec): K3, (k2tog, k5) 8 (6) times, (k2tog, k6) 35 (43) times, (k2tog, k5) 7 (5) times, k2tog, k2.

6th, 7th and 8th sizes only
Next round (Dec): K3, (k2tog, k6) 3 (8, 15) times, (k2tog, k5) 57 (51, 39) times, (k2tog, k6) 3 (8, 15) times, k2tog, k2.

9th size only
Next round (Dec): K2, (k2tog, k5) 34 times, (k2tog, k4) 12 times, (k2tog, k5) 34 times, k2tog, k2.

All sizes
31 (40, 43, 51, 55, 64, 68, 70, 81) sts dec, 277 (294, 325, 341, 373, 390, 424, 450, 473) sts.

Work 4 (5, 6, 8, 10, 12, 13, 14, 17) rounds straight.

1st size only
Next round (Dec): K3, k2tog, k6, * k2tog, k7; rep from * to last 5 sts, k2tog, k3.

2nd size only
Next round (Dec): K3, (k2tog, k5) 9 times, (k2tog, k6) 21 times, (k2tog, k5) 8 times, k2tog, k2.

3rd size only
Next round (Dec): K3, (k2tog, k6) 12 times, (k2tog, k5) 18 times, (k2tog, k6) 12 times, k2tog, k2.

4th and 5th sizes only
Next round (Dec): K2, (k2tog, k4) 8 (6) times, (k2tog, k5) 35 (43) times, (k2tog, k4) 7 (5) times, k2tog, k2.

6th, 7th and 8th sizes only
Next round (Dec): K2, (k2tog, k5) 6 (8, 18) times, (k2tog, k4) 50 (51, 32) times, (k2tog, k5) 6 (8, 18) times, k2tog, k2.

9th size only
Next round (Dec): K2, (k2tog, k4) 34 times, (k2tog, k3) 12 times, (k2tog, k4) 34 times, k2tog, k1.

All sizes
31 (39, 43, 51, 55, 63, 68, 69, 81) sts dec, 246 (255, 282, 290, 318, 327, 356, 381, 392) sts.

Work 2 (2, 3, 3, 4, 6, 9, 9, 8) rounds straight.

1st size only
Next round (Dec): * K2tog, k6; rep from * to last 6 sts, k6.

2nd size only
Next round (Dec): K2, (k2tog, k4) 9 times, (k2tog, k5) 21 times, (k2tog, k4) 8 times, k2tog, k2.

3rd size only
Next round (Dec): K2, (k2tog, k5) 15 times, (k2tog, k4) 11 times, (k2tog, k5) 15 times, k2tog, k2.

4th, 5th, 6th, 7th and 8th sizes only
Next round (Dec): K2, (k2tog, k4) 20 (24, 6, 8, 18) times, (k2tog, k3) 9 (5, 50, 51, 32) times, (k2tog, k4) 20 (24, 6, 8, 18) times, k2tog, k1.

9th size only
Next round (Dec): K1, (k2tog, k3) 36 times, (k2tog, k2) 7 times, (k2tog, k3) 36 times, k2tog, k1.

All sizes
30 (39, 42, 50, 54, 63, 68, 69, 80) sts dec, 216 (216, 240, 240, 264, 264, 288, 312, 312) sts.
Work 1 round straight.

Short Row Section
Next row (RS): K to 8 sts after marker (left front), w&t.
Next row (WS): P to 8 sts after marker (right front), w&t.
Next row: K to 6 (6, 6, 6, 7, 7, 8, 8, 9) sts before last turn, w&t.
Next row: P to 6 (6, 6, 6, 7, 7, 8, 8, 9) sts before last turn, w&t.
Repeat last 2 rows twice more, knitting back to beginning of round marker after last turn.
Next round: K to end, reconciling w&ts and removing additional markers as you work – leaving beginning of round marker in place.

Place Yoke Chart

This section is worked in the round. Use either the chart or written instructions provided.

Commencing with line 1 of Yoke Chart, work 12 st patt rep 18 (18, 20, 20, 22, 22, 24, 26, 26) times across round.

Continue in this manner until all 39 lines of chart have been completed.

You will work decreases on line 21 to give 180 (180, 200, 200, 220, 220, 240, 260, 260) sts, on line 29 to give 144 (144, 160, 160, 176, 176, 192, 208, 208) sts and finally on line 39 to give 108 (108, 120, 120, 132, 132, 144, 156, 156) sts.

Yoke Chart is now complete.

Neckband

Change to smaller circular needle (40–60cm in length).

Next round: * K2, p2; rep from * to end of round.

Repeat this round until neckband measures approximately 2cm (¾in) from cast-on edge.

Cast off in rib.

FINISHING

Graft together the 2 sets of 6 (8, 8, 10, 10, 12, 12, 14, 14) sts held on waste yarn at each underarm.

Soak in lukewarm soapy water, rinse if required, then pin out to size and leave to dry flat.

Darn in any ends.

WRITTEN INSTRUCTIONS FOR CHART

YOKE CHART

Round 1: K1, yo, skp, k7, k2tog, yo.

Round 2 and all even-numbered rounds except round 18: Knit.

Round 3: K1, yo, k1, skp, k5, k2tog, k1, yo.

Round 5: K1, yo, k2, skp, k3, k2tog, k2, yo.

Round 7: K1, yo, k3, skp, k1, k2tog, k3, yo.

Round 9: K1, yo, k4, sk2p, k4, yo.

Round 11: K4, k2tog, yo, k1, yo, skp, k3.

Round 13: K3, k2tog, (k1, yo) twice, k1, skp, k2.

Round 15: K2, k2tog, k2, yo, k1, yo, k2, skp, k1.

Round 17: K1, k2tog, k3, yo, k1, yo, k3, skp.

Round 18: Knit to within last st of round, pm for new BOR.

Round 19: Removing previous BOR marker at start of round, sk2p, k4, yo, k1, yo, k4.

Round 21 (Dec): K1, skp, k7, k2tog.

Round 23: K1, yo, skp, k5, k2tog, yo.

Round 25: K1, yo, k1, skp, k3, k2tog, k1, yo.

Round 27: K1, yo, k2, skp, k1, k2tog, k2, yo.

Round 29 (Dec): K4, sk2p, k3.

Round 31: K2, k2tog, yo, k1, yo, skp, k1.

Round 33: K1, k2tog, (k1, yo) twice, k1, skp.

Round 35: K1, k2tog, (k1, yo) twice, k1, skp.

Round 37: K1, k2tog, (k1, yo) twice, k1, skp.

Round 39 (Dec): K1, k2tog, k3, skp.

CHART NOTES

This lace pattern has a decrease which uses a stitch from the previous round in order to align the patterning correctly.

Round 18: Follow chart as set to last stitch.

Round 19: Work first sk2p using the un-worked stitch from previous round, then continue following chart as set.

Ensure the end of round marker is positioned immediately before the decrease.

Yoke Chart

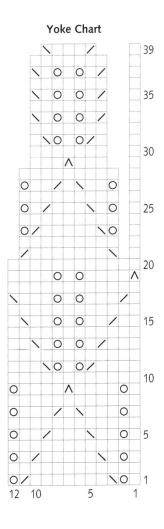

Key

 knit

 k2tog

skp

yo

sk2p

Denby

The original inspiration for Denby came from Twageos from The Vintage Shetland Project, a dramatic over-sized tam; which features a multitude of motifs and a four-shade colour palette. My goal was to create a pared-down, simplified, easily-worn hat that 'nodded' to Twageos but was a significantly different and original design.

I found one of the motifs in Twageos particularly inspirational – an abstract 8-petal flower motif that seems distinctly reminiscent of the decoration found on Denby pottery; in particular the hand-sponged flowers on 1970s dinner sets. I decided to highlight this stunning motif by using it in isolation on Denby; working with just two shades across the entire hat, I further emphasised the drama of this striking pattern.

The hat follows a simple construction commencing with a 2 × 2 ribbed brim, which is folded over to create a frame to the face whilst also providing extra warmth over the ears and around the back of the neck. The body of the hat is knitted in stranded colourwork throughout, and is a great introduction to stranded colourwork and an enjoyable knit for more experienced Fair Isle knitters. I use the two-handed stranded colourwork method, holding one colour in each hand, picking the colour held in my left hand and throwing the colour held in my right.

I have provided multiple variations in this one simple pattern, first of all by offering two colourway options: Colourway A uses cool 'pottery-esque' shades of Excelana 4 Ply with Himalayan Blue as the accent colour against the neutral background of Limestone. Colourway B reverses this with neutral Limestone as the foreground and with a darker shade, Dark as Night, as the background. These two chart variations give lots of scope for trying different colour combinations. In addition the pattern offers two styles; a fitted beanie style or a longer, slouchy version. Choose the relevant chart for the hat length and colourway you wish to knit. The colourwork sections of the pattern are charted with each line read from right to left and repeated around the hat.

Denby

YARN

Susan Crawford Excelana 4 Ply, 100% British wool (159m / 174yds per 50g skein)

Colourway A

1 skein, shade Limestone – Yarn A

1 skein, shade Himalayan Blue – Yarn B

Colourway B

1 skein, shade Dark as Night – Yarn A

1 skein, shade Limestone – Yarn B

Yarn kits available from susancrawfordvintage.com

GAUGE

29 sts and 32 rounds = 10cm (4in) over stranded colourwork worked in the round, after blocking.

We obtained this gauge using 3.25mm needles.

If necessary use an alternative needle size to obtain the correct gauge.

SUGGESTED NEEDLES

Small needles: 2.75mm (US 2) circular needle (40cm in length)

Large needles: 3.25mm (US 3) circular needle (40cm in length)

Set of 3.25mm (US 3) DPNs

NOTIONS

Stitch markers

Pom pom maker (optional)

SAMPLE SHOWN

Denby is modelled by Susan, who is wearing the 2nd size beanie and the 3rd size slouchy versions of the hat. Susan has a 50cm (20in) head circumference.

SIZING AND FINISHING GUIDE

The measurements given represent the dimensions of the knitting after finishing and blocking according to the pattern instructions. The schematic and the measurements should be used to assist in the blocking process to ensure the finished piece is the correct size. Measurements are given in centimetres with inches shown in parentheses.

	1st Size	2nd Size	3rd Size
To fit head circumference	45–50 (18–20)	50–55 (20–22)	55–60 (22–24)

Finished Measurements

Beanie

u Height without brim	16½ (6½)	16½ (6½)	16½ (6½)
w Height with brim (folded)	20½ (8¼)	20½ (8¼)	20½ (8¼)
x Circumference at widest point	43½ (17½)	49½ (19¾)	56 (22½)

Slouchy

u Height without brim	21½ (8½)	21½ (8½)	21½ (8½)
w Height with brim (folded)	25½ (10¼)	25½ (10¼)	25½ (10¼)
x Circumference at widest point	43½ (17½)	49½ (19¾)	56 (22½)

SCHEMATIC

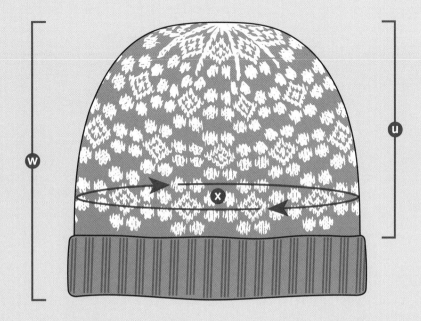

Colourway A

BRIM

Using smaller circular needle and yarn B, cast on 124 (144, 152) sts. Join into a round, taking care not to twist work, pm to indicate end of round.

RIBBING

Round 1: * K2, p2; rep from * to end of round.
Repeat this round until ribbing measures 4cm (1½in) from cast-on edge.
Next round: Work as set by pattern, placing a removable stitch marker at beginning of this round to indicate fold line. Continue as set by pattern until ribbing measures 8cm (3¾in) from cast-on edge.

Change to larger circular needle and yarn A.

Colourway B

BRIM

Using smaller circular needle and yarn A, cast on 124 (144, 152) sts. Join into a round, taking care not to twist work, pm to indicate end of round.

RIBBING

Round 1: * K2, p2; rep from * to end of round.
Repeat this round until ribbing measures 4cm (1½in) from cast-on edge.
Next round: Work as set by pattern, placing a removable stitch marker at beginning of this round to indicate fold line. Continue as set by pattern until ribbing measures 8cm (3¾in) from cast-on edge.

Change to larger circular needle.

Both Colourways

1st size only
Next round (Inc): Using yarn A, k1, m1, k to last st, m1, k1; 126 sts.

2nd size only
Next round: Using yarn A, k to end of round.

3rd size only
Next round (Inc): Using yarn A, k1, * m1, k15; rep from * to last st, k1; 162 sts.

All sizes
Place Chart
Knit all rounds to produce colourwork as follows:
Next round: Commencing with line 1, work correct chart for colourway and height 7 (8, 9) times across round.
Continue as set until line 51 (68) of Beanie (Slouchy) Chart is completed, working crown decreases as indicated and changing to DPNs when needed; 14 (16, 18) sts.

Break yarn and draw through remaining sts. Pull tightly and thread yarn through centre of hat to WS.

FINISHING
Soak hat in lukewarm soapy water, rinse if required. Fold brim to outside of hat along fold line and remove marker, then dry on a balloon or a head form. Darn in all remaining ends.

Make a Pom Pom (Optional)
Using yarn B and a 6½cm (2½in) pom pom maker (or cut two pieces of cardboard into circles of the same diameter with a central hole), wind on a combination of shades as preferred to make a pom pom approximately 7cm (2¾in) in diameter. Leave long ends on the yarn used to tie and secure the pom pom, then use these to attach it at the centre top of the hat.

Slouchy

Beanie

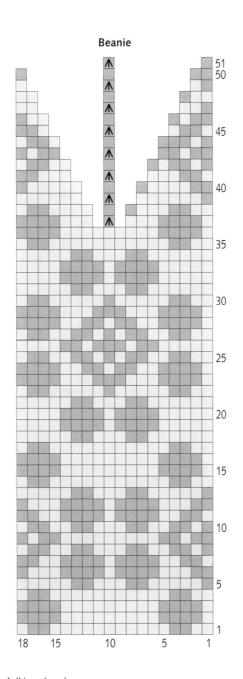

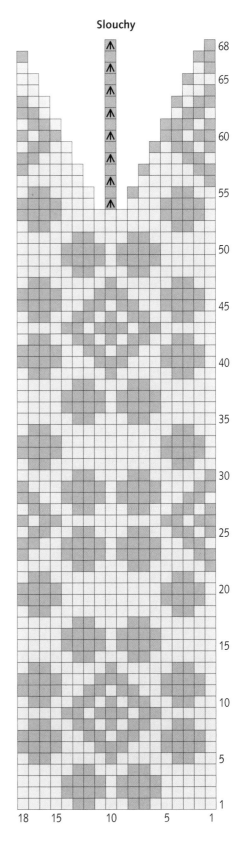

Key

☐ Yarn A (Limestone)

■ Yarn B (Himalayan Blue)

⋀ cdd

Colourway B

Beanie

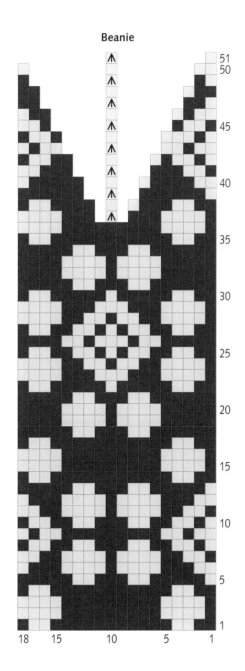

Slouchy

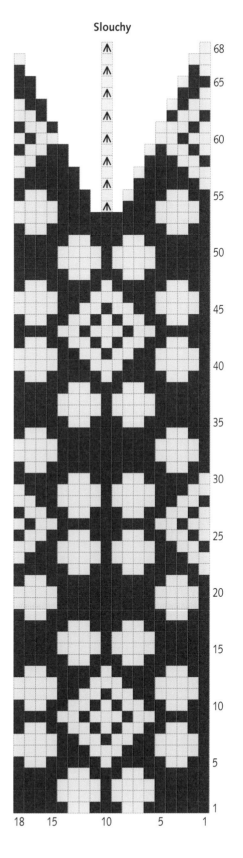

Key

■ Yarn A (Dark As Night)

□ Yarn B (Limestone)

∧ cdd

···· EVOLUTION ····

Floribunda

Floribunda was inspired by the Rose Cardigan from The Vintage Shetland Project, which featured a rose motif repeating around the cardigan in bands, first of red then of pink. On some rounds three colours had to be worked to create this beautiful motif with the pattern repeating over the entire garment. I decided to use this motif but simplify it slightly so that only two colours are ever worked on any one round and placed the motifs in a traditional yoke setting with decreases placed between the motifs.

Floribunda is knitted in Barn, a DK weight yarn, spun from a blend of Jacobs and Shetland fleeces, creating a light natural grey shade. It is knitted from the bottom up commencing with a twisted rib, a steek is then added at the centre front and the cardigan body is then worked simply with every round knitted. On reaching the underarm the work is set aside and the sleeves also knitted in the round. The three pieces are then all joined together. Shaping is worked at this point creating attractive 'fully-fashioned' detailing. Short rows are worked across the back of the cardigan to ensure the neck fits well and then the yoke is worked using three gorgeous shades of Barn, hand dyed in true 'rose-like' shades.

The cardigan is designed to have a slightly loose, comfortable fit, but the underarm shaping ensures that the yoke fits neatly on the shoulders. It is designed to be worn with 13–19cm (5¼–7½in) of positive ease.

All charts are read from right to left on every round.

Floribunda

YARN

Susan Crawford Barn

100% British wool, a unique blend of Jacob, white Shetland and black Shetland fleeces,

DK weight (225m / 246yds per 100g skein approx)

4 (4, 5, 5, 6, 7, 7, 8, 8) 100g skeins, shade Dry Stone Wall – Yarn A

2 (2, 2, 2, 2, 3, 3, 3, 3) 10g skeins, shade Rosehip – Yarn B

2 (2, 2, 3, 3, 3, 3, 3, 4) 10g skeins, shade Cottage Rose – Yarn C

1 (2, 2, 2, 2, 2, 2, 2, 3) 10g skeins, shade Folius – Yarn D

Yarn kits available from susancrawfordvintage.com

GAUGE

20 sts and 26 rounds = 10cm (4in) over stocking stitch and stranded colourwork, worked in the round.

We obtained this gauge using 4.5mm needles.

If necessary use an alternative needle size to obtain the correct gauge.

SUGGESTED NEEDLES

Small needles: 3.75mm (US 5) circular needle (80–100cm in length)

 Set of 3.75mm (US 5) DPNs

Large needles: 4.5mm (US 7) circular needle (40cm in length)

 4.5mm (US 7) circular needle (80–100cm in length)

 Set of 4.5mm (US 7) DPNs

NOTIONS

Waste yarn or stitch holders

Stitch markers

9 buttons approx 1½cm (½in) diameter

Sewing needle and matching thread

1½m (60in) of coordinating ribbon approx 1½cm (½in) wide (optional)

SAMPLE SHOWN

Floribunda is modelled by Susan who is wearing the 4th size, with 19cm (7½in) of ease.

SIZING AND FINISHING GUIDE

Choose the 'To fit' size closest to your actual chest measurement when deciding which size to knit, bearing in mind the fit you would like to achieve. Use in conjunction with the Schematic to identify which size you should knit.

The measurements given represent the dimensions of the knitting after finishing and blocking according to the pattern instructions and will help you identify which size you should knit. They can also be used to help make adjustments to the finished size of your knitting if needed. The Schematic and the measurements should be used to assist in the pinning-out process to ensure the finished piece is the correct size. Measurements are given in centimetres with inches shown in parentheses.

	1st Size	2nd Size	3rd Size	4th Size	5th Size	6th Size	7th Size	8th Size	9th Size
To fit chest	71–76 (28–30)	81–86 (32–34)	91–97 (36–38)	102–107 (40–42)	112–117 (44–46)	122–127 (48–50)	132–137 (52–54)	142–147 (56–58)	152–157 (60–62)
Finished Measurements									
a Chest circumference (fastened)	89 (35¾)	99 (39¾)	109 (43¾)	119 (47¾)	129 (51¾)	139 (55¾)	149 (59¾)	159 (63¾)	169 (67¾)
b Length to underarm	27½ (11)	29 (11½)	29 (11½)	29½ (11¾)	30½ (12¼)	30½ (12¼)	31½ (12½)	31½ (12½)	32½ (13)
c Yoke depth	19 (7½)	19½ (7¾)	21 (8½)	21½ (8¾)	24 (9½)	26 (10½)	27½ (11)	28 (11¼)	30 (12)
d Finished length	46½ (18½)	48½ (19¼)	50 (20)	51 (20½)	54½ (21¾)	56½ (22¾)	59 (23½)	59½ (23¾)	62½ (25)
g Neck circumference	58 (23¼)	58 (23¼)	63 (25¼)	68 (27¼)	73 (29¼)	73 (29¼)	78 (31¼)	83 (31¼)	83 (33¼)
h Sleeve length	43 (17¼)	43 (17¼)	44 (17½)	44 (17½)	45 (18)	45 (18)	46 (18½)	46 (18½)	47 (19)
m Upper arm circumference	30 (12)	32 (12¾)	35 (14)	37 (14¾)	40 (16)	43 (17¼)	46 (18½)	49 (19½)	52 (20¾)

SCHEMATIC

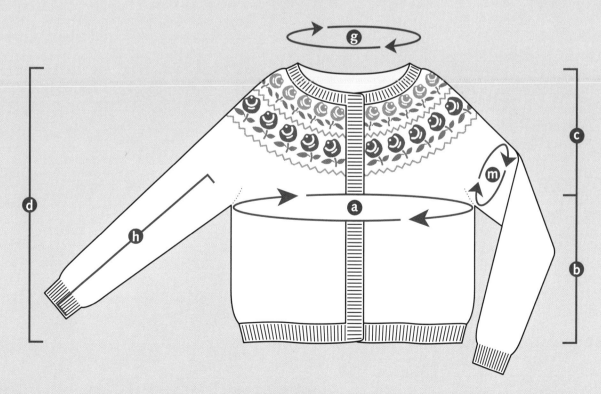

DIRECTIONS

BODY

Using smaller circular needle (80–100cm) and yarn A, cast on 173 (193, 213, 233, 253, 273, 293, 313, 333) sts using long tail cast-on method.

Welt

Worked back and forth.

Next row (RS): * K1tbl, p1; rep from * to last st, k1tbl.

Next row (WS): * P1, k1; rep from * to last st, k1.

Repeat this round until ribbing measures 5cm (2in).

Lower Body (worked in the round)

Change to larger circular needle (80–100cm).

Commence working in stocking stitch (knit every round), inserting steek as follows.

Next round: Cast on 8 sts using backward loop method, k across these cast-on sts, pm after 4 sts worked to indicate end of round, k1, m1, then k to end of round; 182 (202, 222, 242, 262, 282, 302, 322, 342) sts.

Next round: K 47 (52, 57, 62, 67, 72, 77, 82, 87), pm to indicate first side seam, k a further 88 (98, 108, 118, 128, 138, 148, 158, 168) sts, pm to indicate second side seam, k to end of round.

Next round: K to end of round.

Continue as set by last round until work measures 27½ (29, 29, 29½, 30½, 30½, 31½, 31½, 32½) cm (11, 11½, 11½, 11¾, 12¼, 12¼, 12½, 12½, 13 in), or desired length from cast-on edge.

Armhole divide

Next round: * K to 3 (4, 4, 5, 5, 6, 6, 7, 7) sts beyond next marker, place last 6 (8, 8, 10, 10, 12, 12, 14, 14) sts worked onto waste yarn, removing marker; rep from * once more, k to end of round; 12 (16, 16, 20, 20, 24, 24, 28, 28) sts dec, 170 (186, 206, 222, 242, 258, 278, 294, 314) sts.

Yours sts will now be divided as follows: 44 (48, 53, 57, 62, 66, 71, 75, 80) sts (including 4 steek sts, on each front and 82 (90, 100, 108, 118, 126, 136, 144, 154) sts on back.

SLEEVES

Using smaller DPNs and yarn A, cast on 44 (44, 48, 48, 52, 52, 56, 56, 60) sts using long tail cast-on method. Join into a round taking care not to twist sts, placing a marker to indicate beginning of round.

Cuff

Next round: * K1tbl, p1; rep from * to end of round.

Repeat this round until cuff measures 5cm (2in) from cast-on edge.

Change to larger DPNs.

Next round (Inc): K1, m1, k to 1 st before marker, m1, k1; 2 sts dec, 46 (46, 50, 50, 54, 54, 58, 58, 62) sts.

K 12 (9, 8, 7, 6, 5, 5, 4, 4) rounds.

Next round (Inc): K1, m1, k to 1 st before marker, m1, k1; 2 sts inc.

Repeat last 13 (10, 9, 8, 7, 6, 6, 5, 5) rounds a further 6 (8, 9, 11, 12, 15, 16, 19, 20) times; 60 (64, 70, 74, 80, 86, 92, 98, 104) sts.

Work with further shaping until sleeve measures 43 (43, 44, 44, 45, 45, 46, 46, 47) cm (17¼, 17¼, 17½, 17½, 18, 18, 18½, 18½, 19 in) from cast-on edge.

Armhole Divide

Without working, move sts around on needle, placing last 3 (4, 4, 5, 5, 6, 6, 7, 7) sts before marker and first 3 (4, 4, 5, 5, 6, 6, 7, 7) sts after marker onto waste yarn, removing marker. Break yarn; 54 (56, 62, 64, 70, 74, 80, 84, 90) sts.

JOIN YOKE

Using larger circular needle and yarn A attached at end of round, k across 44 (48, 53, 57, 62, 66, 71, 75, 80) sts on right front, pm, k across 54 (56, 62, 64, 70, 74, 80, 84, 90) sts on first sleeve, pm, k across 82 (90, 100, 108, 118, 126, 136, 144, 154) sts on back, pm, then k across 54 (56, 62, 64, 70, 74, 80, 84, 90) sts on second sleeve, pm, then k across 44 (48, 53, 57, 62, 66, 71, 75, 80) sts on left front; 278 (298, 330, 350, 382, 406, 438, 462, 494) sts.

Next round: K to end of round.

Next round (Dec): * K to 3 sts before marker, skp, k1, sm, k1, k2tog; rep from * a further 3 times, k to end of round; 8 sts dec.

Repeat this round a further 6 (5, 9, 9, 9, 9, 10, 13, 14) times; 222 (250, 250, 270, 302, 326, 350, 350, 374) sts.

Your sts will now be divided as follows: 37 (42, 43, 47, 52, 56, 60, 61, 65) sts for each front (including 4 steek stitches), 40 (44, 42, 44, 50, 54, 58, 56, 60) sts for each sleeve, and 68 (78, 80, 88, 98, 106, 114, 116, 124) sts for back.

1st and 6th sizes only

Next round (Dec): K to second marker (right back), sm, k1, k2tog, k 29 (48), skp, k2tog, k to 3 sts before marker, skp, k1, sm, k to end of round; 4 sts dec, 218 (322) sts.

2nd, 3rd and 5th sizes only

Next round (Dec): K to 3 sts before second marker (right back), skp, k1, sm, k1, k2tog, k 34 (35, 44), skp, k2tog, k to 3 sts before marker, skp, k1, sm, k1, k2tog, k to end of round; 6 sts dec, 244 (244, 296) sts.

7th and 8th sizes only

Next round (Dec): * K to second marker (right back), sm, k1, k2tog, k to 3 sts before next marker, k2tog, k to end of round; 2 sts dec, (348, 348) sts.

All sizes

K 0 (2, 2, 4, 10, 14, 17, 16, 21) rounds without further shaping; 218 (244, 244, 270, 296, 322, 348, 348, 374) sts.

Short Row Section

Next row (RS): K to 8 sts after 4th (left front) marker, w&t.

Next row (WS): P to 8 sts after 4th (right front) marker, w&t.

Next row: K to 6 (6, 6, 6, 7, 7, 8, 8, 9) sts before last turn, w&t.

Next row: P to 6 (6, 6, 6, 7, 7, 8, 8, 9) sts before last turn, w&t.

Repeat last 2 rows twice more. Then knit back to end of round marker after last turn, reconciling w&ts.

Next round: K to end, reconciling w&ts and removing additional markers as you work – leaving beginning of round marker in place.

Place Charts

Commencing with line 1 of Charts, work sts 1-4 of Steek Chart, then work st 1 of Yoke Chart, followed by working marked repeat 16 (18, 18, 20, 22, 24, 26, 26, 28) times across round, then work st 15 once, followed by sts 5-8 of Steek Chart. Continue in this manner until all 40 lines of charts have been completed.

You will work decreases on line 24 to give 186 (208, 208, 230, 252, 274, 296, 296, 318) sts and on line 40 to give 122 (136, 136, 150, 164, 178, 192, 192, 206) sts. Yoke and Steek Charts are now complete.

1st size only

Next round (Dec): Using yarn A, k59, skp, k2tog, k to end of round; 2 sts dec, 120 sts.

2nd, 4th, 5th, 6th and 9th sizes only

Next round (Dec): Using yarn A, k 10 (5, 8, 9, 16), * skp, k 6 (15, 10, 4, 3); rep from * a further 6 (3, 5, 12, 16) times, then work skp, k2tog, ** k 6 (15, 10, 4, 3), k2tog; rep from ** to last 10 (5, 8, 9, 16) sts, k to end of round; 16 (10, 14, 28, 36) sts dec, 120 (140, 150, 150, 170) sts.

3rd, 7th and 8th sizes only

Next round (Dec): Using yarn A, k4, * skp, k 29 (4, 7); rep from * a further 1 (14, 9) times, then work skp, k2tog, ** k 29 (4, 7), k2tog; rep from ** to last 4 sts, k to end of round; 6 (32, 22) sts dec, 130 (160, 170) sts.

All Sizes

Neck Band (Worked back and forth)

Change to smaller circular needle.

Next row (RS, Dec): Using yarn A throughout, cast off 4 steek sts removing marker (1 st on RH needle), p2tog, k1tbl, * p1, k1tbl; rep from * to last 4 sts, then cast off 4 remaining steek sts; 9 sts dec, 111 (111, 121, 131, 141, 141, 151, 161, 161) sts.

Next row (WS): With WS facing, rejoin yarn A. * P1, k1; rep from * to last st, p1.

Next row (RS): * K1tbl, p1; rep from * to last st, k1tbl.

Repeat last two rows until neck band measures 2cm (¾in) ending with a WS row.

Next row (RS): Cast off in k1, p1 rib.

FRONT BANDS

Reinforce steek before cutting open. Cut open steek.

Left Front Button Band

Using smaller needle and yarn A, and commencing at upper edge of neck band with RS facing, pick up and k 97 (99, 105, 105, 113, 117, 123, 125, 131) sts evenly down length of cardigan front; this is approx 4 sts for every 5 rows.

Next row (WS): * P1, k1; rep from * to last st, p1.

Next row (RS): * K1tbl, p1; rep from * to last st, k1tbl.

Repeat these 2 rows until band measures 3cm (1¼in) from picked up edge ending with a WS row. Cast off in k1, p1 rib.

Right Front Buttonhole Band

Using smaller needle and yarn A and commencing at bottom edge of welt with RS facing, pick up and k 97 (99, 105, 105, 113, 117, 123, 125, 131) sts evenly up length of cardigan front; this is approx 4 sts for every 5 rows.

Next row (WS): * P1, k1; rep from * to last st, p1.

Next row (RS): * K1tbl, p1; rep from * to last st, k1tbl.

Repeat these 2 rows once more, then work WS row only once more again.

Buttonhole row 1 (RS): Patt 4 (5, 4, 4, 4, 6, 5, 6, 5) sts, * cast off following 2 sts (leaves 1 st on RH needle), patt a further 8 (8, 9, 9, 10, 10, 11, 11, 12) sts; rep from * a further 7 times, cast off following 2 sts (leaves 1 st on RH needle), patt 2 (3, 2, 2, 2, 4, 3, 4, 3) sts.

Buttonhole row 2 (WS): Patt 3 (4, 3, 3, 3, 5, 4, 5, 4) sts, * turn and cast on 2 sts using cable cast-on bringing yarn forward between 2 cast-on sts before placing 2nd cast-on st onto needle, turn, patt to next set of cast-off sts; rep from * a further 7 times, turn and cast on 2 sts using cable cast-on and bringing yarn forward between 2 cast-on sts before placing 2nd cast-on st onto needle, patt 4 (5, 4, 4, 4, 6, 5, 6, 5) sts.

Continue in twisted ribbing until band measures 3cm (1¼in) ending with a WS row. Using larger needle, cast off in rib.

FINISHING

Graft together the 2 sets of 6 (8, 8, 10, 10, 12, 12, 14, 14) sts held on waste yarn at each underarm.

Soak sweater in lukewarm soapy water, rinse if required, then pin out to size and leave to dry flat. Trim raw edge of steek back to 2 sts width. Darn in any ends.

If desired, pin ribbon along length of each button band commencing below ribbed neck band, concealing raw edge of steek and ensuring the pick-up row of the button band is centred beneath the ribbon. Stitch ribbon in place with slip stitch using matching sewing thread.

Sew buttons in position in line with corresponding buttonholes.

Steek   **Yoke Chart**   **Steek**

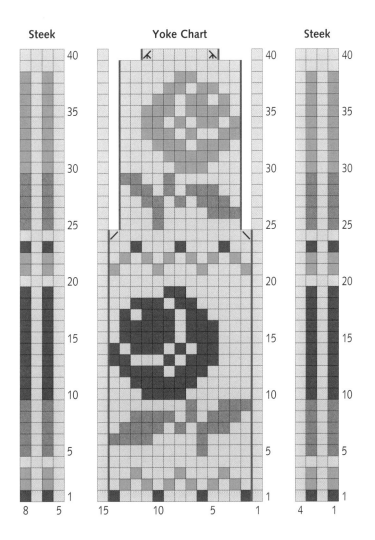

40   40   40

35   35   35

30   30   30

25   25   25

20   20   20

15   15   15

10   10   10

5   5   5

1   1   1

8   5   15   10   5   1   4   1

Key

Yarn A (Dry Stone Wall)

Yarn B (Rosehip)

Yarn C (Cottage Rose)

Yarn D (Foljus)

/ k2tog

\ skp

k3tog

sk2p

Pattern repeat

···· EVOLUTION ····

Gallica

The inspiration for Gallica is multifaceted – like most designs in reality. Inspired in part by Harriet, the charming pair of mittens in The Vintage Shetland Project; the motifs on those mittens is in turn inspired by the floral motifs popular in the late 1940s and early 1950s, just like the Rose Cardigan and indeed, Floribunda. Using one motif all-over the design was suggested to me by Stromfirth, the striking 'shooting' stockings from The Vintage Shetland Project. These too use a floral inspired motif across the body and foot of the sock and use just two colours throughout. I decided to pare down the floral motif into a more abstract, cubist design but instead of only using two shades throughout, I used five.

The colour scheme was, quite obviously, inspired by the gorgeous shades of the Floribunda cardigan. When hand dyeing those shades, I discovered that if I continued using the dye bath continuously without adding more dye it achieved the vibrant and glorious pink shade of Gallica and the almost apple-like shade of Frond. Bordering these with their sister shades of Rosehip and Folius added depth and variation and created a wonderfully tonal surface pattern. These colours against the natural grey of the Barn yarn gives the mittens a real vintage quality, a favourite pair of mittens found in the drawer of an old wooden cabinet.

The mittens are knitted in the round using DPNs, or magic loop could be used if preferred. The knitting commences with the cuff which is worked in striped corrugated ribbing as do many traditional Shetland knits. The main hand of the mitten is worked in standard stranded colour work with only ever two colours used on any one round and a maximum of 5 stitches in any one colour at a time. The thumb gusset is worked to the side of the mitten. Additional thumb gusset stitches are worked by knitting into the front and back of the stitches as shown in the charts. To ensure continuity of the pattern you may need to knit into the back of the stitch with a different colour than that used to knit into the front of the stitch. Be sure to follow the chart which indicates which shade to use for each part of the increase. The two mittens are knitted identically.

There are three mitten sizes each with its own chart and all the charts are read from right to left on every round. There are also three Thumb Charts provided alongside the main mitten charts.

Gallica

YARN

Susan Crawford Barn

100% British wool, a unique blend of Jacob, white Shetland and black Shetland fleeces,

DK weight (225m / 246yds per 100g skein approx)

1 (1, 1) skein, shade Dry Stone Wall – Yarn A

3 (3, 3) 10g skeins, shade Frond – Yarn B

1 (1, 1) 10g skeins, shade Folius – Yarn C

2 (3, 3) 10g skeins, shade Gallica – Yarn D

1 (2, 2) 10g skeins, shade Rosehip – Yarn E

Yarn kits available from susancrawfordvintage.com

GAUGE

26 sts and 28 rounds = 10cm (4in) over stranded colourwork, worked in the round. We obtained this gauge using 3.5mm needles.

If necessary use an alternative needle size to obtain the correct gauge.

SUGGESTED NEEDLES

Small needles: Set of 2.75mm (US 2) DPNs

Large needles: Set of 3.5mm (US 4) DPNs

NOTIONS

Waste yarn or stitch holders

Stitch markers

SAMPLE SHOWN

Susan is wearing the 2nd size mittens in the photographs.

SIZING AND FINISHING GUIDE

The measurements given represent the dimensions of the knitting after finishing and blocking according to the pattern instructions. The schematic and the measurements should be used to assist in the pinning-out / blocking process to ensure the finished piece is the correct size. Measurements are given in centimetres with inches shown in parenthesis.

		1st size	2nd size	3rd size
To fit		16½–17½ (6½–7)	18–19½ (7¼–7¾)	20–22 (8–8¾)

Finished Measurements

		1st size	2nd size	3rd size
k	Cuff length	7 (2¾)	7 (2¾)	7 (2¾)
l	Mitten length (with cuff)	25½ (10¼)	27 (10¾)	28½ (11½)
m	Mitten circumference	21½ (8½)	21½ (8½)	24½ (9¾)
u	Mitten length to tip (without cuff)	18½ (7½)	20 (8)	21½ (8½)
v	Thumb length to tip	6 (2½)	7 (2¾)	7½ (3)

SCHEMATIC

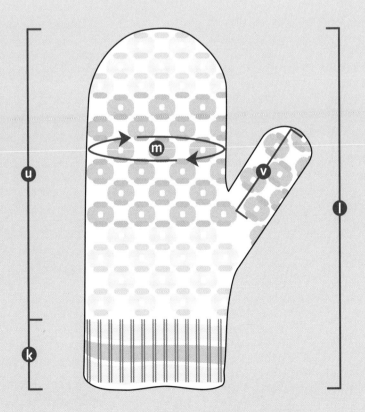

DIRECTIONS

LEFT MITTEN

Cuff

Using smaller DPNs and yarn A, cast on 58 (58, 66) sts using long tail cast-on method. Join into round, taking care not to twist cast-on sts. Place marker to indicate end of round.

Rounds 1, 2, 3 & 4: * K1A, p1B; rep from * to end of round.
Rounds 5, 6, 7 & 8: * K1A, p1D; rep from * to end of round.
Rounds 9, 10, 11 & 12: * K1A, p1B; rep from * to end of round.

Hand

Change to larger DPNs.
Next round: Using yarn A, k to end of round.

3rd size only
Next 2 rounds: Using yarn A, k to end of round.

All sizes
Place Chart

Commencing with line 1 of Mitten Chart for the size you are making, patt to end of round. Continue in this manner until line 8 (8, 8) has been completed.

Insert Thumb Gusset

Next round (Inc): Maintaining patt, work 28 (28, 32) sts, pm, (kfb) twice, pm, patt 28 (28, 32) sts; 2 sts inc.
Continue as set by Mitten Chart, working increases as indicated until round 22 (22, 22) has been completed and there are 16 (16, 16) sts between markers.

Next round (Dec): Work as set by line 23 (23, 23) of Mitten Chart to first marker, remove marker and place 16 (16, 16) thumb sts onto waste yarn, sm, and patt to end of round; 56 (56, 64) sts.

Commencing with line 24 (24, 24), work as set by Mitten Chart until line 42 (46, 50) has been completed.

Shape Top

Next round (Dec): Maintaining patt as set by Mitten Chart, * skp, patt to 2 sts before marker, k2tog, sm; rep from * once more; 4 sts dec.
Continue as set by last round until line 52 (56, 60) of Mitten Chart has been completed; 16 (16, 24) sts.

Join Mitten Top

Divide 8 (8, 12) sts from front and back onto 2 DPNs and using a third DPN work three needle cast-off on the RS of mitten as follows:
Next row: K2togA, k2togB, 2 sts on RH DPN, pass first st worked over second st to cast off, * k2togA, 2 sts on RH DPN, pass first st worked over second st to cast off, k2togB, 2 sts on RH DPN, pass first st worked over second st to cast off; rep from * to end of row, break both yarns and draw through final loop.
Place each tail on tapestry needle in turn and thread through to WS of mitten. Secure in place on WS of work.

THUMB

1st & 2nd sizes only
Using larger DPNs and working from line 1 of Thumb Chart for the size you are making, work across 16 (16) sts held on waste yarn, using yarn A, pick up 2 sts across opening, pm; 18 (18) sts.

3rd size only
Using larger DPNs and working from line 1 of 3rd Size Thumb Chart, work across 16 sts held on waste yarn, m1 using yard D, pick up 2 sts across opening using yarn A, then m1 using yarn A, pm; 20 sts.

All sizes
Commencing with line 2 of Thumb Chart, work as set until line 16 (18, 20) has been completed.

Shape Top

Next round (Dec): Using yarn A, * k2tog * rep from * to end of round; 9 (9, 10) sts.

Break yarn, leaving a long end. Thread yarn through remaining 9 (9, 10) sts, draw up tightly, then take yarn to WS of thumb and darn in end.

RIGHT MITTEN

Work exactly as Left Mitten.

FINISHING

Turn mitten to WS and darn in all ends. Turn to RS. Soak in lukewarm soapy water, rinse if required, then block using mitten stretcher if possible. Alternatively leave to dry flat.

Mitten Chart

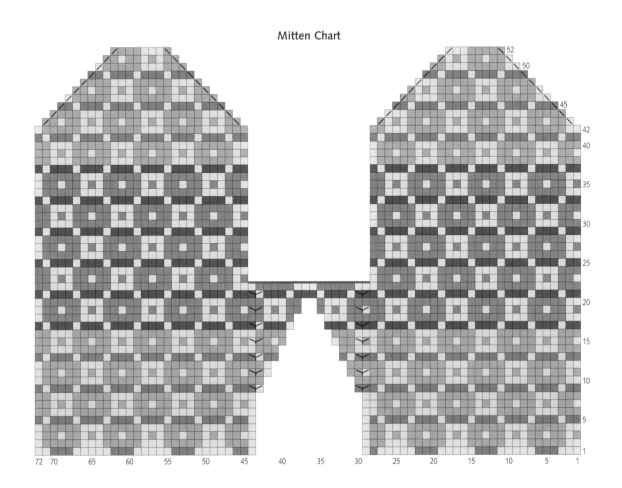

Thumb Chart

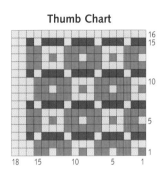

Key

☐	Yarn A (Dry Stone Wall)
▨	Yarn B (Frond)
▨	Yarn C (Folius)
▨	Yarn D (Gallica)
■	Yarn E (Rosehip)
⋎	knit into front and back
◥	skp
◢	k2tog
—	Thumb stitches

Mitten Chart

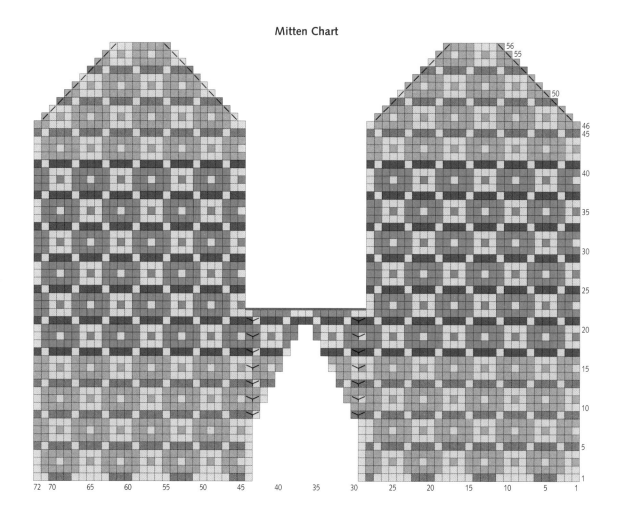

Thumb Chart

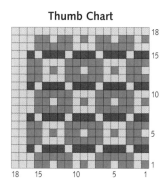

Key

 Yarn A (Dry Stone Wall)

Yarn B (Frond)

Yarn C (Folius)

Yarn D (Gallica)

Yarn E (Rosehip)

⊻ knit into front and back

◣ skp

◥ k2tog

— Thumb stitches

Mitten Chart

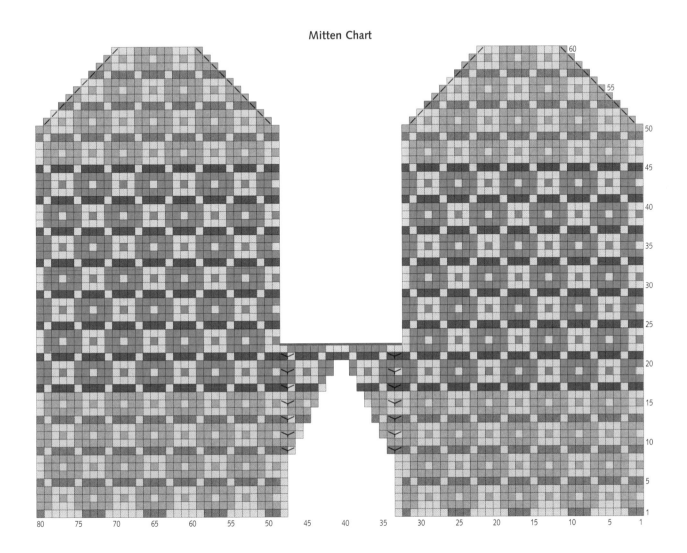

Thumb Chart

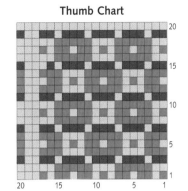

Key

 Yarn A (Dry Stone Wall)

Yarn B (Frond)

Yarn C (Folius)

Yarn D (Gallica)

Yarn E (Rosehip)

knit into front and back

skp

k2tog

— Thumb stitches

Umbel

This stunning design uses a number of traditional Shetland lace patterns within a contemporary, elegant shawl. The shawl starts with just 3 stitches at its narrowest point and is worked from that point as an asymmetric triangle with increases worked on every right side row at one edge only. A garter stitch border is worked at either edge at the same time, removing any need to knit a border once the body of the shawl is completed. Once the required number of stitches has been reached, the decorative lace sections are worked in turn, creating an eye-catching shawl which is surprisingly easy to knit and wonderful to wear. All the individual sections of the pattern have both charted and written instructions with all partial repeats included. In addition all wrong side rows are purl rows and 5mm needles are used throughout making it a very quick knit too.

The shawl is knitted in Excelana 4 Ply creating a soft but defined fabric with drape but some structure as with all Shetland shawls, meaning the shawl can be accurately blocked and will hold its shape and size. To minimise joins I have used the 'spit-splice' method when joining in each new ball, resulting in only 2 ends, one at the very beginning and one at the very end. If you don't use this method, there is ample wool within the 5 skeins recommended in the pattern, to introduce yarn at row ends.

Written instructions are provided as an alternative to the charts. All charts are read from right to left on RS rows and left to right on WS rows.

Umbel

Susan Crawford Excelana 4 Ply, 100% British wool (159m / 174yds per 50g skein)

5 skeins, shade Agapanthus

Yarn kits available from susancrawfordvintage.com

GAUGE

36 sts and 40 rows = 10cm (4in) over main lace pattern (Chart A), after blocking.

We used a 5mm circular needle to obtain this gauge.

18 sts and 20 rows = 10cm (4in) over decorative lace panels (Chart F or H), after blocking.

We used a 5mm circular needle to obtain this gauge.

If necessary use an alternative needle size to obtain the correct gauge.

SUGGESTED NEEDLES

5mm (US 8) circular needle (80–100cm in length)

NOTIONS

Stitch markers

116 ···· EVOLUTION ····

SIZING AND FINISHING GUIDE

The measurements given represent the dimensions of the knitting after finishing and blocking according to the pattern instructions. The Schematic and the measurements should be used to assist in the pinning-out process to ensure the finished piece is the correct size. Measurements are given in centimetres with inches shown in parentheses.

Finished Measurements

d Length   180
                       (72)

w Width   120
                       (48)

F Wingspan   220
                       (88)

SCHEMATIC

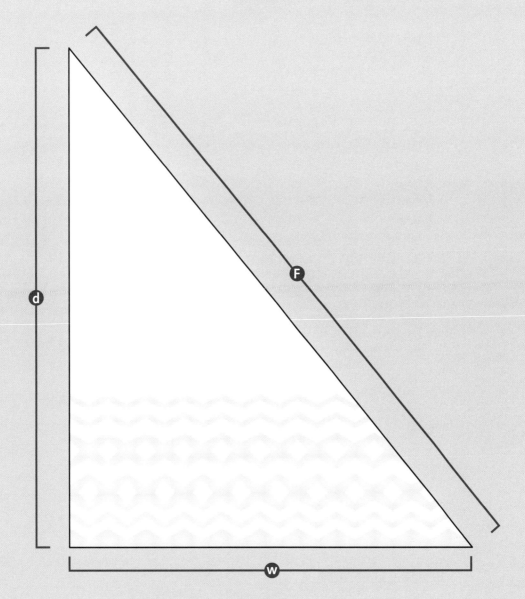

DIRECTIONS

SET-UP
Using appropriate needle to obtain gauge, cast on 3 sts using long-tail cast-on method.
Next row (WS): K3.

Place Garter Stitch Border
Row 1 (RS, Inc): K1, m1f, k1, m1f, k1; 2 sts inc, 5 sts.
Row 2 (WS): K2, p1, k2.
Row 3 (Inc): K2, m1f, k1, m1f, k2; 2 sts inc, 7 sts.
Row 4: K3, pm, p1, pm, k3.
Row 5 (Inc): K3, sm, k1, m1f, sm, k3; 1 st inc, 8 sts.
Row 6: K3, p2, k3.
Row 7 (Inc): K3, sm, k2, m1f, sm, k3; 1 st inc, 9 sts.
Row 8: K3, p3, k3.
Row 9 (Inc): K3, sm, k3, m1f, sm, k3; 1 st inc, 10 sts.
Row 10: K3, p4, k3.
Row 11 (Inc): K3, sm, k4, m1f, sm, k3; 1 st inc, 11 sts.
Row 12: K3, p5, k3.

COMMENCE MAIN LACE PATTERN
Commence with the Main Lace as directed below, using either the charts or the written instructions provided.

Chart A
Commencing with line 1, work Chart A across all sts, inc 1 st on each RS row. Continue in this manner until all 12 lines have been completed; 6 sts inc, 17 sts.
Repeat lines 5–12 only a further 29 times until 133 sts on needle (including garter st edging), then repeat lines 5–8 only once more; 135 sts. Your sts will be divided as follows: 3 garter edging sts, 129 patt sts, 3 garter edging sts.

Chart B
Commencing with line 1, work Chart B across all sts. Continue in this manner until both lines have been completed.

Chart C
Commencing with line 1, work Chart C across all sts, inc 1 st on each RS row. Continue in this manner until all 12 lines have been completed; 6 sts inc, 141 sts. Your sts will be divided as follows: 3 garter edging sts, 135 patt sts, 3 garter edging sts.

Chart D
Commencing with line 1, work Chart D across all sts, inc 1 st on each RS row. Continue in this manner until all 4 lines have been completed; 2 sts inc, 143 sts. Your sts will be divided as follows: 3 garter edging sts, 137 patt sts, 3 garter edging sts.

Chart E
Commencing with line 1, work Chart E across all sts, inc 1 st on each RS row. Continue in this manner until all 12 lines have been completed; 6 sts inc, 149 sts. Your sts will be divided as follows: 3 garter edging sts, 143 patt sts, 3 garter edging sts.

Chart D
Commencing with line 1, work Chart D across all sts, inc 1 st on each RS row. Continue in this manner until all 4 lines have been completed; 2 sts inc, 151 sts. Your sts will be divided as follows: 3 garter edging sts, 145 patt sts, 3 garter edging sts.

COMMENCE DECORATIVE LACE PANELS
Commence with the Decorative Lace as directed below, using either the charts or the written instructions provided.

Chart F
Commencing with line 1, work Chart F across all sts, inc 1 st on each RS row. Continue in this manner until all 22 lines have been completed; 11 sts inc, 162 sts. Your sts will be divided as follows: 3 garter edging sts, 156 patt sts, 3 garter edging sts.

Chart G
Commencing with line 1, work Chart G across all sts, inc 1 st on each RS row. Continue in this manner until all 6 lines have been completed; 3 sts inc, 165 sts. Your sts will be divided as follows: 3 garter edging sts, 159 patt sts, 3 garter edging sts.

Chart D
Commencing with line 1, work Chart D across all sts, inc 1 st on each RS row. Continue in this manner until all 4 rows have been completed; 2 sts inc, 167 sts. Your sts will be divided as follows: 3 garter edging sts, 161 patt sts, 3 garter edging sts.

Chart H
Commencing with line 1, work Chart H across all sts, inc 2 sts on first row and then 1 st on each following RS row. Continue in this manner until all 22 lines have been completed; 12 sts inc, 179 sts. Your sts will be divided as follows: 3 garter edging sts, 173 patt sts, 3 garter edging sts.

Chart J

Commencing with line 1, work Chart J across all sts, inc 1 st on each RS row. Continue in this manner until all 12 lines have been completed; 6 sts inc, 185 sts. Your sts will be divided as follows: 3 garter edging sts, 179 patt sts, 3 garter edging sts.

Chart K

Commencing with line 1, work Chart K across all sts, inc 1 st on each RS row. Continue in this manner until all 12 lines have been completed; 6 sts inc, 191 sts. Your sts will be divided as follows: 3 garter edging sts, 185 patt sts, 3 garter edging sts.

Next row (RS, Inc): K to last 3 sts, m1f, k3; 192 sts.
Next row (WS): K3, p to last 3 sts, k3.
Next row (Inc): K to last 3 sts, m1f, k3; 193 sts.

Garter Stitch Edging

Next row (WS): K to end of row.
Next row (RS): K to end of row.
Next row: K to end of row.
Loosely cast off all sts.

FINISHING

Soak in lukewarm soapy water, rinse if required and then carefully pin out to size as indicated on the schematic on a flat absorbent surface. Ensure edges are straight and all lace sections are evenly 'blocked out'. Leave to dry completely. Darn in any ends.

CHART A

Row 1 (RS, Inc): K4, yo, sk2p, yo, k1, m1f, k3; 1 st inc, 12 sts.

Row 2 and all WS rows: K3, p to last 3 sts, k3.

Row 3 (Inc): K3, k2tog, yo, k1, yo, k2tog, k1, m1f, k3; 1 st inc, 13 sts.

Row 5 (Inc): K4, * yo, sk2p, yo, k1; rep from * to last 5 sts, yo, k2tog, m1f, k3; 1 st inc.

Row 7 (Inc): K3, k2tog, yo, k1, * yo, sk2p, yo, k1; rep from * to last 4 sts, k1, m1f, k3; 1 st inc.

Row 9 (Inc): K4, * yo, sk2p, yo, k1; rep from * to last 3 sts, m1f, k3; 1 st inc.

Row 11 (Inc): K3, k2tog, yo, k1, * yo, sk2p, yo, k1; rep from * to last 6 sts, yo, k2tog, k1, m1f, k3; 1 st inc.

Row 12: K3, p to last 3 sts, k3.

CHART B

Row 1 (RS): K4, * yo, sk2p, yo, k1; rep from * to last 3 sts, k3.

Row 2 (WS): K3, p to last 3 sts, k3.

CHART C

Row 1 (RS, Inc): K2, * k4, (yo, sk2p, yo, k1) three times; rep from * to last 5 sts, k2, m1f, k3; 1 st inc, 136 sts.

Row 2 and all WS rows: K3, p to last 3 sts, k3.

Row 3 (Inc): * K8, (yo, sk2p, yo, k1) twice; rep from * to last 8 sts, k5, m1f, k3; 1 st inc, 137 sts.

Row 5 (Inc): * K10, yo, sk2p, yo, k3; rep from * to last 9 sts, k6, m1f, k3; 1 st inc, 138 sts.

Row 7 (Inc): K4, yo, k2tog, * k11, k2tog, yo, k1, yo, k2tog; rep from * to last 4 sts, k1, m1f, k3; 1 st inc, 139 sts.

Row 9 (Inc): K3, k2tog, yo, k1, yo, k2tog, * k7, k2tog, yo, k1, yo, sk2p, yo, k1, yo, k2tog; rep from * to last 3 sts, m1f, k3; 1 st inc, 140 sts.

Row 11 (Inc): K4, yo, sk2p, yo, * k1, yo, k2tog, k3, k2tog, yo, (k1, yo, sk2p, yo) twice; rep from * to last 5 sts, k2, m1f, k3; 1 st inc, 141 sts.

Row 12: K3, p to last 3 sts, k3.

CHART D

Row 1 (RS, Inc): K3, k2tog, yo, * k1, yo, sk2p, yo; rep from * to last 4 sts, k1, m1f, k3; 1 st inc.

Row 2 (WS): K3, p to last 3 sts, k3.

Row 3 (Inc): K3, * k1, yo, sk2p, yo; rep from * to last 3 sts, m1f, k3; 1 st inc.

Row 4: K3, p to last 3 sts, k3

CHART E

Row 1 (RS, Inc): K6, * (yo, sk2p, yo, k1) three times, k4; rep from * to last 9 sts, yo, sk2p, yo, k3, m1f, k3; 1 st inc, 144 sts.

Row 2 and all WS rows: K3, p to last 3 sts, k3.

Row 3 (Inc): K8, * (yo, sk2p, yo, k1) twice, k8; rep from * to last 8 sts, yo, sk2p, yo, k2, m1f, k3; 1 st inc, 145 sts.

Row 5 (Inc): K10, * yo, sk2p, yo, k13; rep from * to last 7 sts, yo, sk2p, yo, k1, m1f, k3; 1 st inc, 146 sts.

Row 7 (Inc): K4, yo, k2tog, * k11, k2tog, yo, k1, yo, k2tog); rep from * to last 12 sts, k9, m1f, k3; 1 st inc, 147 sts.

Row 9 (Inc): K3, k2tog, yo, k1, yo, k2tog, * k7, k2tog, yo, k1, yo, sk2p, yo, k1, yo, k2tog; rep from * to last 11 sts, k8, m1f, k3; 1 st inc, 148 sts.

Row 11 (Inc): K4, yo, sk2p, yo, k1, yo, k2tog, * k3, k2tog, yo, (k1, yo, sk2p, yo) twice, k1, yo, k2tog; rep from * to last 10 sts, k3, k2tog, yo, k2, m1f, k3; 1 st inc, 149 sts.

Row 12: K3, p to last 3 sts, k3.

CHART F

Row 1 (RS, Inc): K2, * k4, (yo, sk2p, yo, k1) three times: rep from * to last 5 sts, k2, m1f, k3; 1 st inc, 152 sts.

Row 2 and all WS rows: K3, p to last 3 sts, k3.

Row 3 (Inc): * K8, (yo, sk2p, yo, k1) twice; rep from * to last 8 sts, k5, m1f, k3; 1 st inc, 153 sts.

Row 5: K6, * k4, yo, sk2p, yo, k9; rep from * to last 3 sts, m1f, k3; 1 st inc, 154 sts.

Row 7 (Inc): K4, yo, k2tog, * k11, k2tog, yo, k1, yo, k2tog; rep from * to last 4 sts, k1, m1f, k3; 1 st inc, 155 sts.

Row 9 (Inc): K5, yo, k2tog, * k9, k2tog, yo, k3, yo, k2tog; rep from * to last 4 sts, k1, m1f, k3; 1 st inc, 156 sts.

Row 11 (Inc): K4, k2tog, yo, k1, yo, k2tog, * k4, (k1, k2tog, yo, k1, yo, k2tog) twice; rep from * to last 3 sts, m1f, k3; 1 st inc, 157 sts.

Row 13 (Inc): K3, k2tog, yo, k3, yo, k2tog, * k3, k2tog, yo, k3, yo, sk2p, yo, k3, yo, k2tog; rep from * to last 3 sts, m1f, k3; 1 st inc, 158 sts.

Row 15 (Inc): K4, yo, k2tog, k1, k2tog, yo, k1 * k4, (yo, k2tog, k1, k2tog, yo, k1) twice; rep from * to last 4 sts, k1, m1f, k3; 1 st inc, 159 sts.

Row 17 (Inc): K5, yo, sk2p, yo, k4, * (k3, yo, sk2p, yo) twice, k4; rep from * to last 3 sts, m1f, k3; 1 st inc, 160 sts.

Row 19 (Inc): K4, k2tog, yo, * k11, yo, k2tog, k1, k2tog, yo; rep from * to last 10 sts, k7, m1f, k3; 1 st inc, 161 sts.

Row 21 (Inc): K3, k2tog, yo, * k13, yo, sk2p, yo; rep from * to last 12 sts, k9, m1f, k3; 1 st inc, 162 sts.

Row 22: K3, p to last 3 sts, k3.

CHART G

Row 1 (RS, Inc): K9, k2tog, yo, k1, yo, k2tog, * k11, k2tog, yo, k1, yo, k2tog; rep from * to last 4 sts, k1, m1f, k3; 1 st inc, 163 sts.

Row 2 and all WS rows: K3, p to last 3 sts, k3.

Row 3 (Inc): * K7, k2tog, yo, k1, yo, sk2p, yo, k1, yo, k2tog; rep from * to last 3 sts, m1f, k3; 1 st inc, 164 sts.

Row 5 (Inc): K5, * k2tog, yo, (k1, yo, sk2p, yo) twice, k1, yo, k2tog, k3; rep from * to last 15 sts, k2tog, yo, (k1, yo, sk2p, yo) twice, k2, m1f, k3; 1 st inc, 165 sts.

Row 6: K3, p to last 3 sts, k3.

CHART H

Row 1 (RS, Inc): K3, k2tog, yo, k1, yo, sk2p, yo, k5, * (yo, sk2p, yo, k1) three times, k4; rep from * to last 9 sts, yo, sk2p, yo, k1, yo, k2, m1f, k3; 2 sts inc, 169 sts.

Row 2 and all WS rows: K3, p to last 3 sts, k3.

Row 3 (Inc): K5, k2tog, yo, k9, * (yo, sk2p, yo, k1) twice, k8; rep from * to last 9 sts, yo, sk2p, yo, k1, yo, k2tog, m1f, k3; 1 st inc, 170 sts.

Row 5 (Inc): K5, * k13, yo, sk2p, yo; rep from * to last 5 sts, k2, m1f, k3; 1 st inc, 171 sts.

Row 7 (Inc): * K10, yo, sk2p, yo, k3, rep from * to last 11 sts, k8, m1f, k3; 1 st inc, 172 sts.

Row 9 (Inc): K9, * yo, k2tog, k1, k2tog, yo, k11; rep from * to last 3 sts, m1f, k3; 1 st inc, 173 sts.

Row 11 (Inc): K8, * yo, k2tog, yo, sk2p, yo, k2tog, yo, k9; rep from * to last 5 sts, yo, k2tog, m1f, k3; 1 st inc, 174 sts.

Row 13 (Inc): K7, * (yo, k2tog) twice, k1, (k2tog, yo) twice, k7; rep from * to last 7 sts, (yo, k2tog) twice, m1f, k3; 1 st inc, 175 sts.

Row 15 (Inc): K8, * yo, k2tog, yo, sk2p, yo, k2tog, yo, k9; rep from * to last 7 sts, (yo, k2tog) twice, m1f, k3; 1 st inc, 176 sts.

Row 17 (Inc): K9, * yo, k2tog, k1, k2tog, yo, k11; rep from * to last 7 sts, yo, k2tog, k2, m1f, k3; 1 st inc, 177 sts.

Row 19 (Inc): K10, * yo, sk2p, yo, k13; rep from * to last 7 sts, yo, sk2p, yo, k1, m1f, k3; 1 st inc, 178 sts.

Row 21 (Inc): K10, * k2tog, yo, k14; rep from * to last 8 sts, k2tog, yo, k3, m1f, k3; 1 st inc, 179 sts.

Row 22: K3, p to last 3 sts, k3.

CHART J

Row 1 (RS, Inc): K4, yo, k2tog, * k11, k2tog, yo, k1, yo, k2tog; rep from * to last 13 sts, k10, m1f, k3; 1 st inc, 180 sts.

Row 2 and all WS rows: K3, p to last 3 sts, k3.

Row 3 (Inc): K3, k2tog, yo, k1, yo, k2tog, * k7, k2tog, yo, k1, yo, sk2p, yo, k1, yo, k2tog; rep from * to last 12 sts, k9, m1f, k3; 1 st inc, 181 sts.

Row 5 (Inc): K4, yo, sk2p, yo, k1, yo, k2tog, k3, * k2tog, yo, (k1, yo, sk2p, yo) twice, k1, yo, k2tog, k3; rep from * to last 8 sts, k2tog, yo, k1, yo, k2tog, m1f, k3; 1 st inc, 182 sts.

Row 7 (Inc): K2, * k4, (yo, sk2p, yo, k1) three times; rep from * to last 4 sts, k1, m1f, k3; 1 st inc, 183 sts.

Row 9 (Inc): * K8, (yo, sk2p, yo, k1) twice: rep from * to last 7 sts, k4, m1f, k3; 1 st inc, 184 sts.

Row 11 (Inc): * K10, yo, sk2p, yo, k3; rep from * to last 8 sts, k5, m1f, k3; 1 st inc, 185 sts.

Row 12: K3, p to last 3 sts, k3.

CHART K

Row 1 (RS, Inc): K4, yo, k2tog, * k11, k2tog, yo, k1, yo, k2tog; rep from * to last 3 sts, m1f, k3; 1 st inc, 186 sts.

Row 2 and all WS rows: K3, p to last 3 sts, k3.

Row 3 (Inc): K3, k2tog, yo, k1, * yo, k2tog, k7, k2tog, yo, k1, yo, sk2p, yo, k1; rep from * to last 4 sts, k1, m1f, k3; 1 st inc, 187 sts.

Row 5 (Inc): K4, yo, sk2p, yo, k1, * yo, k2tog, k3, k2tog, yo, k1, (yo, sk2p, yo, k1) twice; rep from * to last 3 sts, m1f, k3; 1 st inc, 188 sts.

Row 7 (Inc): K6, * (yo, sk2p, yo, k1) three time, k4; rep from * to last 6 sts, yo, sk2p, yo, m1f, k3; 1 st inc, 189 sts.

Row 9 (Inc): K8, * (yo, sk2p, yo, k1) twice, k8; rep from * to last 5 sts, yo, k2tog, m1f, k3; 1 st inc, 190 sts.

Row 11 (Inc): K10, * yo, sk2p, yo, k13; rep from * to last 4 sts, k1, m1f, k3; 1 st inc, 191 sts.

Row 12: K3, p to last 3 sts, k3.

Chart A

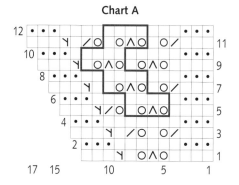

Chart B

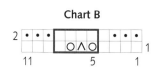

Chart C

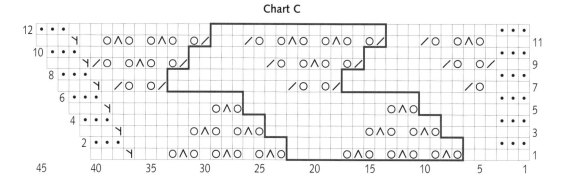

Chart D

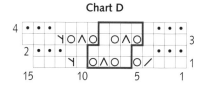

Chart E

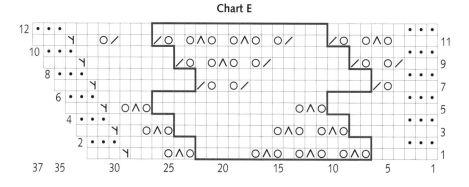

Key

k on RS, p on WS

• p on RS, k on WS (garter stitch edge)

O yo

∧ sk2p

╱ k2tog

Υ m1f

☐ Pattern repeat

Chart F

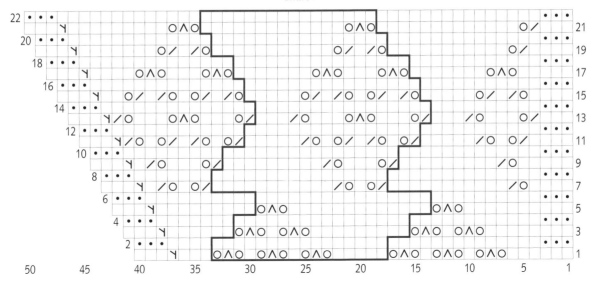

Chart G

Chart H

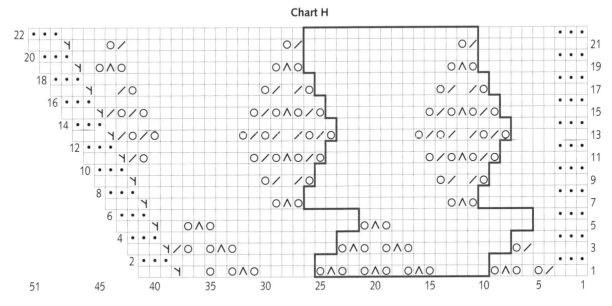

Key

☐	k on RS, p on WS
•	p on RS, k on WS (garter stitch edge)
O	yo
∧	sk2p
⁄	k2tog
Υ	m1f
☐	Pattern repeat

Chart J

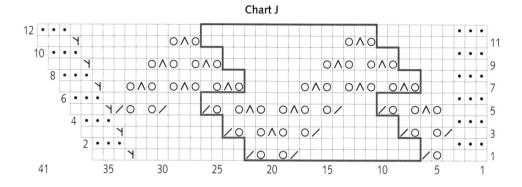

Chart K

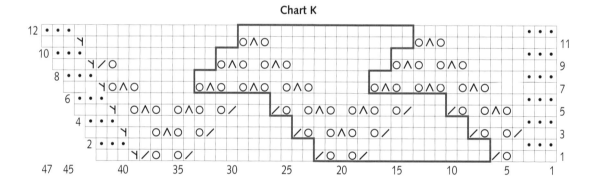

Key

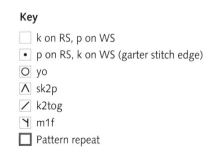

☐ k on RS, p on WS

• p on RS, k on WS (garter stitch edge)

O yo

Λ sk2p

∕ k2tog

Y m1f

☐ Pattern repeat

···· EVOLUTION ····

Lanatus

Fair Isle sweaters are usually seen as heavyweight pieces designed for cold weather wear. However the knitted garments I studied in the Shetland Museum were often lighter weight and suitable for all-year round wear. With Lanatus I wanted to create a similar garment in terms of weight to those I saw at the museum – a Fair Isle sweater that can be worn in warmer weather as well as when temperatures drop. To do this I used Fenella, a fine 2 ply weight wool with the correct properties for stranded colourwork, to create a lightweight garment. I also used a monochrome colour palette inspired by the motifs in Paterson. To create a modern silhouette I decided to knit the top from the neckline down, with short rows worked at the back neck to lower the front neckline. The motifs are worked around the upper body yoke with increases worked on plain knit rows in between. The work is divided at the armhole and a larger needle size is used to create a little more ease.

At this point two versions are available, either continuing to knit the all-over Fair Isle pattern, or instead working in a single colour creating a yoked top with a plain body. In both versions, the needle size is again changed at a recommended point to allow the top to flare very slightly, creating a subtle A-line shape. Working downwards also allows the knitter to decide on finished length to suit their own requirements. Two body length options are included in the pattern. A hip -length option and a more cropped option. After the body is completed the sleeves are also worked downwards, either with matching Fair Isle patterning or knitted plain. The sleeves finish above the elbow and again by using a slightly larger needle, have a little more ease and don't pull in at the cuff.

The colourwork motifs are charted and all charts are read from right to left on every round.

Lanatus is designed to be worn with approximately 10–20cm (4–8in) of positive ease.

Lanatus

YARN

Susan Crawford Fenella 2 Ply, 100% British wool (125m / 136yds per 25g skein)

Version 1: All-over Fair Isle Body

Shorter Length

5 (6, 6, 7, 7, 7, 8, 9, 9) skeins, shade Sloe Gin – Yarn A

4 (5, 5, 5, 6, 6, 6, 7, 8, 8) skeins, shade Balado – Yarn B

Longer Length

5 (6, 6, 7, 7, 7, 8, 9, 9, 10) skeins, shade Sloe Gin – Yarn A

4 (5, 5, 6, 6, 6, 7, 8, 8, 9) skeins, shade Balado – Yarn B

Version 2: Plain Body

Shorter Length

6 (7, 7, 8, 9, 10, 10, 11, 12, 13) skeins, shade Sloe Gin – Yarn A

2 (2, 2, 2, 2, 2, 2, 3, 3) skeins, shade Balado – Yarn B

Longer Length

6 (7, 8, 9, 10, 10, 11, 12, 13, 14) skeins, shade Sloe Gin – Yarn A

2 (2, 2, 2, 2, 2, 3, 3, 3) skeins, shade Balado – Yarn B

Yarn kits available from susancrawfordvintage.com

GAUGE

32 sts and 36 rounds = 10cm (4in) measured over Fair Isle pattern and stocking stitch, worked in the round using size A needles. We obtained this gauge using 3mm needles.

30 sts and 34 rounds = 10cm (4in) measured over both Fair Isle pattern and stocking stitch, worked in the round using size B needles. We obtained this gauge using 3.25mm needles.

28 sts and 32 rounds = 10cm (4in) measured over Fair Isle pattern and stocking stitch, worked in the round using size C needles. We obtained this gauge using 3.5mm needles.

If necessary use an alternative needle size to obtain the correct gauge.

SUGGESTED NEEDLES

Small needles: 2.75mm (US 2) circular needle (40cm in length) or DPNs.
2.75mm (US 2) circular needle (80–100cm in length)

Large needles: **Size A** 3mm (US 2 / 3) circular needle (60cm in length)
3mm (US 2 / 3) circular needle (80–100cm in length)
Size B 3.25mm (US 3) circular needle (40cm in length) or DPNs
3.25mm (US 3) circular needle (80–100cm in length)
Size C 3.5mm (US 4) circular needle (80–100cm in length)

The pattern uses 4 needle sizes progressively increasing. To achieve the best results use mm sized needles.

NOTIONS

Waste yarn or stitch holders
Stitch markers

SAMPLE SHOWN

Lanatus is modelled by Susan wearing version 2 in the 4th size shorter length, with approximately 10cm (4in) of ease; and wearing version 1 also in the 4th size shorter length, knitted in Verdigris and Chalk.

SIZING AND FINISHING GUIDE

Choose the 'To fit' size closest to your actual chest measurement when deciding which size to knit, bearing in mind the fit you would like to achieve. Use in conjunction with the Schematic to identify which size you should knit.

The measurements given represent the dimensions of the knitting after finishing and blocking according to the pattern instructions and will help you identify which size you should knit. They can also be used to help make adjustments to the finished size of your knitting if needed. The Schematic and the measurements should be used to assist in the pinning-out process to ensure the finished piece is the correct size. Measurements are given in centimetres with inches shown in parentheses.

		1st Size	2nd Size	3rd Size	4th Size	5th Size	6th Size	7th Size	8th Size	9th Size	10th Size
	To fit chest	71–76 (28–30)	81–86 (32–34)	91–97 (36–38)	102–107 (40–42)	112–117 (44–46)	122–127 (48–50)	132–137 (52–54)	142–147 (56–58)	152–157 (60–62)	162–167 (64–66)
Finished Measurements											
a	Chest Circumference	92 (36¾)	104 (41½)	112 (44¾)	124 (49½)	136 (54½)	144 (57½)	156 (62½)	168 (67¼)	176 (70½)	188 (75¼)
b	Length to underarm **(Longer length)**	30½ (12¼)	30½ (12¼)	30½ (12¼)	30½ (12¼)	30½ (12¼)	30½ (12¼)	30½ (12¼)	30½ (12¼)	30½ (12¼)	30½ (12¼)
b	Length to underarm **(Shorter length)**	25 (10)	25 (10)	25 (10)	25 (10)	25 (10)	25 (10)	25 (10)	25 (10)	25 (10)	25 (10)
c	Yoke depth	23 (9¼)	23½ (9½)	24 (9¾)	26½ (10¾)	27½ (11)	27½ (11)	28½ (11½)	29 (11¾)	32½ (13)	32½ (13)
d	Total length **(Longer length)**	53½ (21½)	54 (21¾)	54½ (22)	57 (23)	58 (23¼)	58 (23¼)	59 (23¾)	59½ (24)	63 (25¼)	63 (25¼)
d	Total length **(Shorter length)**	48 (19¼)	48½ (19½)	49 (19¾)	51½ (20¾)	52½ (21)	52½ (21)	53½ (21½)	54 (21¾)	57½ (23)	57½ (23)
g	Neck circumference	45 (18)	49 (19½)	52½ (21)	52½ (21)	52½ (21)	54 (21½)	54 (21½)	56½ (22½)	56½ (22½)	56½ (22½)
h	Sleeve length	12½ (5)	12½ (5)	12½ (5)	12½ (5)	12½ (5)	12½ (5)	12½ (5)	12½ (5)	12½ (5)	12½ (5)
m	Upper arm circumference	28 (11¼)	28 (11¼)	32 (12¾)	32 (12¾)	32 (12¾)	36 (14½)	36 (14½)	40 (16)	44 (17½)	52 (20¾)

SCHEMATIC

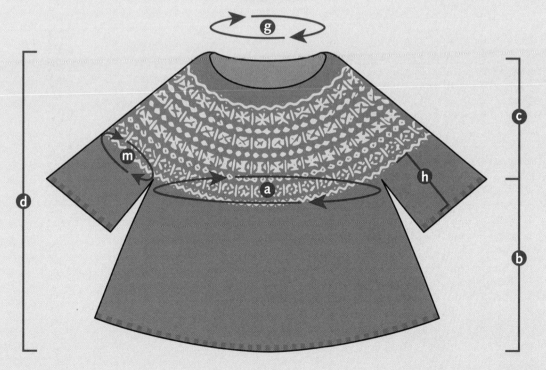

Both Versions

NECK BAND
With smaller circular needle (40cm) and yarn A, cast on 144 (156, 168, 168, 168, 172, 172, 180, 180, 180) sts using a long-tail cast-on. Join into a round taking care not to twist sts, placing a marker to indicate beginning of round.

Round 1: * K2, p2; rep from * to end of round.
Repeat this round until ribbing measures approximately 1cm (½in).
Next round: K to end of round.

Change to size A circular needle (60cm), changing to longer length needle when necessary.

4th and 5th sizes only
Next round (Inc): * K 14 (7), m1; rep from * to end of round; 12 (24) sts inc, 180 (192) sts.
Next round: K to end of round.

6th 7th, 8th, 9th and 10th sizes only
Next round (Inc): K 8 (8, 13, 13, 13), m1, * k5, m1; rep from * to last 9 (9, 12, 12, 12) sts, k to end of round; 32 sts inc, 204 (204, 212, 212, 212) sts.
Next round: K to end of round.

7th, 8th, 9th and 10th sizes only
Next round (Inc): K 11 (14, 14, 14), m1, * k 14 (8, 8, 8), m1; rep from * to last 11 (14, 14, 14) sts, k to end of round; 14 (24, 24, 24) sts inc, 218 (236, 236, 236) sts.

All sizes
Back Neck Shaping
Continuing to use yarn A, commence short row shaping as follows:
Row 1 (RS): K 42 (45, 48, 51, 54, 57, 61, 65, 65, 65), w&t.
Row 2 (WS): P to marker, p 42 (45, 48, 51, 54, 57, 61, 65, 65, 65), w&t.
Row 3: K to 6 sts before wrapped st from last RS row, w&t.
Row 4: P to 6 sts before wrapped st from last WS row, w&t.
Last 2 rows set pattern. Repeat rows 3 and 4 a further 3 (4, 4, 4, 6, 6, 6, 7, 7, 7) times.

Next round (RS, Partial): k to marker.

Next round: K to end of round, reconciling all w&ts as you proceed.

3rd, 4th, 5th and 6th sizes only
Next round: K to end of round.

7th, 8th, 9th and 10th sizes only
Next round: K to end of round.
Next round (Inc): K 4 (0, 0, 16), * k 21 (59, 14, 5), m1; rep from * to last 4 (0, 12, 20) sts, k to end of round; 10 (4, 16, 40) sts inc, 228 (240, 252, 276) sts.
Next round: K to end of round.

All sizes
Place Yoke Chart
Commencing with line 1 of Chart A knit across all sts, working marked pattern repeat 12 (13, 14, 15, 16, 17, 19, 20, 21, 23) times until line 7 of chart has been completed.

First Chart Increase Round
1st and 4th sizes only
Next round (Inc): Using yarn A, * k3, m1; rep from * to end of round; 48 (60) sts inc, 192 (240) sts.

2nd, 3rd, 5th, 6th, 7th, 8th, 9th and 10th sizes only
Next round (Inc): Using yarn A, k 20 (26, 9, 32, 9, 15, 21, 33), m1, * k 2 (2, 3, 2, 3, 3, 3, 3), m1; rep from * to last 18 (24, 6, 30, 6, 12, 18, 30) sts, k to end of round; 60 (60, 60, 72, 72, 72, 72, 72) sts inc, 216 (228, 252, 276, 300, 312, 324, 348) sts.

All sizes
Commencing with line 8 of Chart A work marked pattern repeat 16 (18, 19, 20, 21, 23, 25, 26, 27, 29) times until line 18 of chart has been completed.

Second Chart Increase Round
1st, 4th and 7th sizes only
Next round (Inc): Using yarn A, * k 4 (5, 5), m1; rep from * to end of round; 48 (48, 60) sts inc, 240 (288, 360) sts.

2nd, 3rd, 5th, 6th, 8th, 9th and 10th sizes only
Next round (Inc): Using yarn A, k 16 (22, 10, 33, 16, 22, 34), m1, * k 4 (4, 4, 3, 4, 4, 4), m1; rep from * to last 12 (18, 6, 30, 12, 18, 30) sts, k to end of round; 48 (48, 60, 72, 72, 72, 72) sts inc, 264 (276, 312, 348, 384, 396, 420) sts.

All sizes
Commencing with line 19 of Chart A work marked pattern repeat 20 (22, 23, 24, 26, 29, 30, 32, 33, 35) times until line 25 of chart has been completed.

Third Chart Increase Round

4th size only

Next round (Inc): Using yarn A, * k 6, m1; rep from * to end of round; 48 sts inc, 336 sts.

1st, 2nd, 3rd, 5th, 6th, 7th, 8th, 9th and 10th sizes only

Next round (Inc): Using yarn A, k 18 (17, 23, 18, 13, 19, 17, 23, 35), m1, * k 6 (5, 5, 6, 7, 7, 5, 5, 5), m1; rep from * to last 12 (12, 18, 12, 6, 12, 12, 18, 30) sts, k to end of round; 36 (48, 48, 48, 48, 48, 72, 72, 72) sts inc, 276 (312, 324, 360, 396, 408, 456, 468, 492) sts.

All sizes

Commencing with line 26 of Chart A work marked pattern repeat 23 (26, 27, 28, 30, 33, 34, 38, 39, 41) times until line 36 has been completed.

Fourth Chart Increase Round

Next round (Inc): Using yarn A, k 19 (20, 24, 15, 19, 14, 20, 25, 24, 36), m1, * k 7 (8, 6, 9, 7, 8, 8, 7, 6, 6), m1; rep from * to last 12 (12, 18, 6, 12, 6, 12, 18, 18, 30) sts, k to end of round; 36 (36, 48, 36, 48, 48, 48, 60, 72, 72) sts inc, 312 (348, 372, 372, 408, 444, 456, 516, 540, 564) sts.

Commencing with line 37 of Chart A work marked pattern repeat 26 (29, 31, 31, 34, 37, 38, 43, 45, 47) times until line 43 has been completed.

Fifth Chart Increase Round

Next round (Inc): Using yarn A, k 20 (21, 16, 16, 20, 15, 21, 28, 25, 37), m1, * k 8 (9, 10, 10, 8, 9, 9, 10, 7, 7), m1; rep from * to last 12 (12, 6, 6, 12, 6, 12, 18, 18, 30) sts, k to end of round; 36 (36, 36, 36, 48, 48, 48, 48, 72, 72) sts inc, 348 (384, 408, 408, 456, 492, 504, 564, 612, 636) sts.

Commencing with line 44 of Chart A work marked pattern repeat 29 (32, 34, 34, 38, 41, 42, 47, 51, 53) times until line 54 has been completed.

Sixth Chart Increase Round

Next round (Inc): Using yarn A, k 21 (22, 17, 17, 24, 16, 22, 29, 30, 28), m1, * k 9 (10, 11, 11, 12, 10, 10, 11, 12, 10), m1; rep from * to last 12 (12, 6, 6, 12, 6, 12, 18, 18, 18) sts, k to end of round; 36 (36, 36, 36, 36, 48, 48, 48, 48, 60) sts inc, 384 (420, 444, 444, 492, 540, 552, 612, 660, 696) sts.

Commencing with line 55 of Chart A work marked pattern repeat 32 (35, 37, 37, 41, 45, 46, 51, 55, 58) times until line 61 of chart has been completed.

Seventh Chart Increase Round

1st and 6th sizes only

Next round (Inc): Using yarn A, * k 16 (15), m1; rep from * to end of round; 24 (36) sts inc, 408 (576) sts.

2nd, 3rd, 4th, 5th, 7th, 8th, 9th and 10th sizes only

Next round (Inc): Using yarn A, k 23 (18, 18, 25, 23, 30, 31, 26), m1, * k 11 (12, 12, 13, 11, 12, 13, 14), m1; rep from * to last 12 (6, 6, 12, 12, 18, 18, 12) sts, k to end of round; 36 (36, 36, 36, 48, 48, 48, 48) sts inc, 456 (480, 480, 528, 600, 660, 708, 744) sts.

All sizes

Commencing with line 62 of Chart A work marked pattern repeat 34 (38, 40, 40, 44, 48, 50, 55, 59, 62) times until line 72 of chart has been completed.

Eighth Chart Increase Round

1st, 2nd, 3rd, 5th and 6th sizes only

Next round (Inc): Using yarn A, * k 17 (38, 40, 22, 24), m1; rep from * to end of round; 24 (12, 12, 24, 24) sts inc, 432 (468, 492, 552, 600) sts.

4th, 7th, 8th, 9th and 10th sizes only

Next round (Inc): Using yarn A, k 19 (28, 24, 31, 27), m1, * k 13 (16, 18, 19, 15), m1; rep from * to last 6 (12, 6, 12, 12) sts, k to end of round; 36 (36, 36, 36, 48) sts inc, 516 (636, 696, 744, 792) sts.

Version One – All-over Fair Isle Body

4th, 5th, 6th, 7th and 8th sizes only
Commencing with line 73 of Chart A work marked pattern repeat 43 (46, 50, 53, 58) times until line 79 of chart has been completed.

9th and 10th sizes only
Commencing with line 73 of Chart A work marked pattern repeat 62 (66) times until line 91 of chart has been completed.

Version Two – Plain Body

4th, 5th, 6th, 7th and 8th sizes only
Commencing with line 1 of Chart B work marked pattern repeat 43 (46, 50, 53, 58) times until line 7 of chart has been completed.

9th and 10th sizes only
Commencing with line 73 of Chart A work marked pattern repeat 62 (66) times until line 91 of chart has been completed.

Both Versions

All sizes
Divide Body and Sleeves
Next round: Using yarn A, k 66 (75, 81, 87, 96, 102, 111, 120, 126, 132) back sts, then place following 84 (84, 84, 84, 84, 96, 96, 108, 120, 132) sts on waste yarn for left sleeve, then using backward loop method cast on 6 (6, 6, 12, 12, 12, 12, 12, 12, 18) sts for underarm, k across 132 (150, 162, 174, 192, 204, 222, 240, 252, 264) front sts, then place following 84 (84, 84, 84, 84, 96, 96, 108, 120, 132) sts on waste yarn for right sleeve, then using backward loop method cast on 6 (6, 6, 12, 12, 12, 12, 12, 12, 18) sts for underarm, then k across remaining 66 (75, 81, 87, 96, 102, 111, 120, 126, 132) back sts; 276 (312, 336, 372, 408, 432, 468, 504, 528, 564) body sts.

Version One – All-over Fair Isle Body

Place Body Chart
Change to size B circular needle (80–100cm).
Commencing with line 1 of Chart C knit across all sts, working marked pattern repeat 23 (26, 28, 31, 34, 36, 39, 42, 44, 47) times until line 54 of chart has been completed.

Longer Length
Change to size C circular needle and commencing with line 55 of Chart B continue in pattern until line 98 of chart has been completed.
Using Yarn A, knit 2 rounds.

Shorter Length
Change to size C circular needle and commencing with line 55 of Chart B continue in pattern until line 80 of chart has been completed.
Using Yarn A, knit 1 round.

Version Two – Plain Body
Change to size B circular needle (80–100cm).
Next round: Using yarn A, k to end of round.
Continue as set until 54 rounds have been completed.

Longer Length
Change to size C circular needle and continue in stocking stitch for a further 44 rounds. Alter the number of rounds worked over this section if you wish to alter the final garment length.

Shorter length
Change to size C circular needle and continue in stocking stitch for a further 26 rounds. Alter the number of rounds worked over this section if you wish to alter the final garment length.

Both Versions

WELT
Change to smaller circular needle (80–100cm).
Next round: * K2, p2; rep from * to end of round.
Repeat this round until rib measures 1cm (½in).

SLEEVES
Return 84 (84, 84, 84, 84, 96, 96, 108, 120, 132) sts on waste yarn onto size A circular needle (40cm) or DPNs. Rejoin yarn A and k to end of round, then pick up and k into 6 (6, 12, 12, 12, 12, 12, 12, 12, 24) sts at underarm, placing a marker at centre of underarm sts to indicate beginning of round; 90 (90, 96, 96, 96, 108, 108, 120, 132, 156) sts.

1st and 2nd sizes only
Next round (Partial, Dec): Using A, k3, * k2tog, k12; rep from * to marker; 6 sts dec, 84 sts.

3rd, 4th, 5th, 6th, 7th, 8th, 9th and 10th sizes only
Next round (Partial): Using yarn A, k to marker.

Version One – All-over Fair Isle Sleeves

Place Chart
Change to size B circular needle (40cm) or DPNs. Commencing with line 1 of Chart C knit across all sts, working marked pattern repeat 7 (7, 8, 8, 8, 9, 9, 10, 11, 13) times until line 36 of chart has been completed. Using yarn A, k 2 rounds.

Version Two – Plain Sleeves
Change to size B circular needle (40cm) or DPNs.
Next round: Using yarn A, k to end of round.
Continue as set until 38 rounds have been completed.

Both Versions

CUFF
Change to smaller circular needle (40cm) or DPNs.
Next round: * K2, p2; rep from * to end of round.
Repeat this round until cuff measures 1cm (½in).

FINISHING
Soak sweater in lukewarm soapy water, rinse if required, then pin out to size and dry flat. Darn in any ends.

1st, 2nd & 3rd Sizes

Chart A

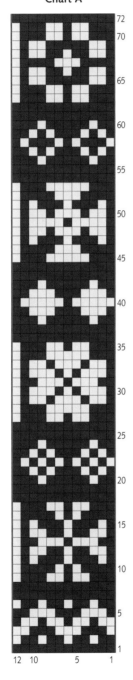

4th, 5th, 6th, 7th & 8th Sizes

Chart A

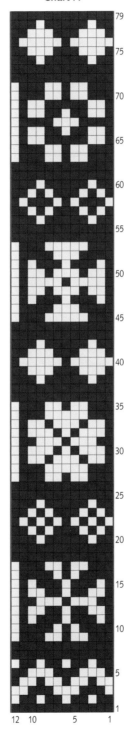

9th & 10th Sizes

Chart A

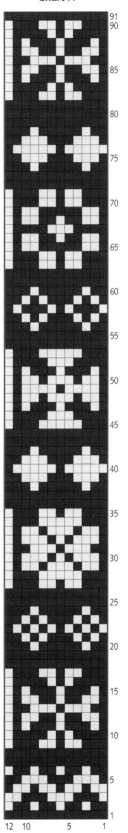

Key

■ Yarn A (Sloe Gin)

▫ Yarn B (Balado)

☐ Pattern repeat

All Sizes
Chart C

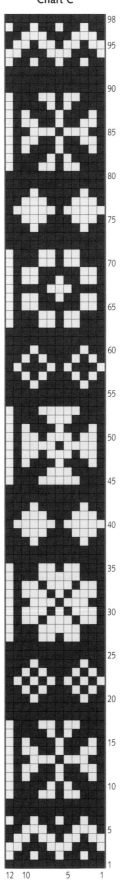

4th, 5th, 6th, 7th & 8th Sizes

Chart B

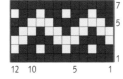

Key

■ Yarn A (Sloe Gin)
□ Yarn B (Balado)
☐ Pattern repeat

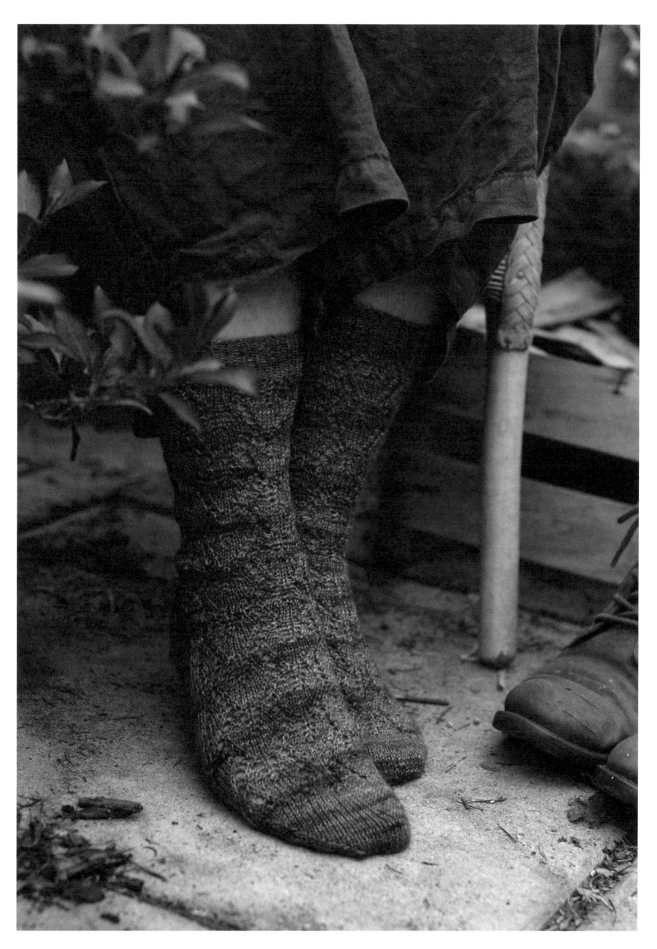

···· EVOLUTION ····

Cloudin

These lacy socks are inspired by the delicate stitch pattern of Johnson from The Vintage Shetland Project. To fit with the dimensions of the sock, I set about customising the lace pattern whilst still retaining the same overall visual effect. Worked on a tight gauge this stitch, whilst being 'lacy', provides a solid fabric for an everyday sock. The socks are worked from the top down with a traditional heel flap, gusset and shaped toe. Once the sock is completed the remaining stitches are grafted together. The lace pattern has tremendous stretch and will look considerably narrower than after it has been blocked.

For the first time, I have been able to use my own sock wool – Bluem Sock. This beautiful yarn is a combination of Bluefaced Leicester wool and nylon, with a tight twist, to create an incredibly soft but robust yarn. This yarn is then hand-dyed in a range of shades, inspired by the landscape around me. The shade I have used is Rolling Mist, a darkish-grey with swirling variations suggesting the mist as it rolls up the hillside at our farm from the river far below.

Explanation is provided in the pattern for adjusting the foot length of your Cloudin socks to achieve a perfect fit. The pattern contains both written and charted instructions for the lace sections. All charts are read from right to left on every round.

Cloudin

YARN
Susan Crawford Bluem Sock, 75% Bluefaced Leicester, 25% Nylon (395m / 432 yds per 100g)
1 skein, shade Rolling Mist
Yarn kits available from susancrawfordvintage.com

GAUGE
34 sts and 48 rounds = 10cm (4in) over lace pattern worked in the round, after blocking.
We obtained this gauge using 2.25mm needles.

If necessary use an alternative needle size to obtain the correct gauge.

SUGGESTED NEEDLES
Set of 2.25mm (US 1) DPNs, or circular needle if preferred

NOTIONS
Stitch markers
Waste yarn

SAMPLE SHOWN
The Cloudin socks are modelled by Susan who is wearing the 2nd size and wears a UK size 7 (EU 41/ US 9.5) shoe.

SIZING AND FINISHING GUIDE

The measurements given represent the dimensions of the knitting after finishing and blocking according to the pattern instructions and will help you identify which size you should knit. They can also be used to help make adjustments to the finished size of your knitting if needed. The Schematic and the measurements should be used to assist in the blocking process to ensure the finished piece is the correct size. Measurements are given in centimetres with inches shown in parentheses.

	1st Size	2nd Size	3rd Size
To fit mid-foot and leg circumference.	20 (8)	23 (9)	25½ (10)

Finished Measurements

		1st Size	2nd Size	3rd Size
p	Leg circumference:	16½ (6½)	19 (7½)	21 (8½)
q	Leg length from cuff to start of heel:	13 (5¼)	16½ (6½)	15½ (6¼)
v	Foot length:	adjustable to fit.		

SCHEMATIC

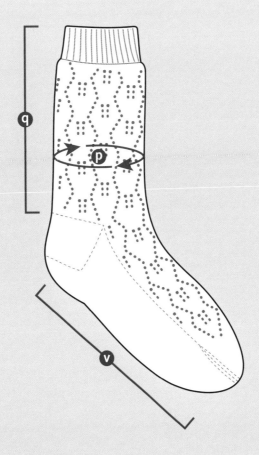

DIRECTIONS

CUFF

Cast on 56 (64, 72) sts using long-tail cast on method.
Join into a round taking care not to twist sts, placing marker to indicate beginning of round.

Round 1: * K1tbl, p1; rep from * to end of round.
This round sets pattern. Repeat this round a further 15 times or until cuff measures 3cm (1¼in)

LEG

Place Chart

Ensure you use correct chart or written instructions for the size you are making,

Next round: Commencing with line 1 of chart, work chart 4 times across all sts.

Continue as set working from chart across all sts until line 12 (16, 20) of chart has been worked.
Repeat lines 1–12 (1–16, 1–20) of chart a further 3 (3, 2) times. To adjust leg length, ensure you end on either line 6 (8, 10) or 12 (16, 20) of chart for size you are making.

HEEL FLAP

Without working, reposition sts, placing last 13 (15, 17) sts worked and the next 14 (16, 18) sts onto one needle and place remaining 29 (33, 37) sts onto waste yarn. Break yarn and with RS facing, rejoin at beginning of work. The heel flap is now worked in rows over these 27 (31, 35) sts.

Next row (RS): * Sl1, k1; rep from * to last st, k1.
Next row (WS): Sl1, p26 (30, 34).
Repeat these 2 rows a further 12 (14, 16 times); 26 (30, 34) rows worked in total.

Turn Heel

Next row (RS): Sl1, k 15 (17, 19), skp, k1, turn.
Next row (WS): Sl1, p6, p2tog, p1, turn.
Next row: Sl1, k to 1 st before gap, skp, k1, turn.
Next row: Sl1, p to 1 st before gap, p2tog, p1, turn.

Continue as set by last 2 rows until all sts have been worked; 17 (19, 21) sts.

GUSSET

Your sock will be knitted in the round from this point. Ensure you continue to use the correct chart or written instructions for the size you are making, starting with the chart line immediately after the last worked round. If you completed the leg with the last line of the chart, start with line 1. If you adjusted leg length ending with line 6 (8, 10) of the chart, start with line 7 (9, 11).

Next round: Sl1, k 16 (18, 20), pick up and k 14 (16, 18) sts along first side of heel flap, pm, then maintaining pattern work chart twice across next 28 (32, 36) sts, k1, pm, then pick up and k 14 (16, 18) sts along remaining side of heel flap, pm for end of round; 74 (84, 94) sts.

Decrease Section

Next round (Dec): K to within 2 sts of first marker, k2tog, sm, work from next line of chart twice across next 28 (32, 36) sts, k1, sm, skp, k to end of round, sm; 2 sts dec.
Next round: K to first marker, sm, work from next line of chart twice across next 28 (32, 36) sts, k1, sm, k to end of round, sm.
Repeat these 2 rounds a further 8 (9, 10) times until a total of 18 (20, 22) sts have been decreased; 56 (64, 72) sts.

FOOT

Next round: K to first marker, sm, work from next line of chart twice across next 28 (32, 36) sts, k1, sm, k to end of round, sm.
Continue as set by this round, repeating lines of chart until foot measures approx 4½ (4½, 5) cm (1¾, 1¾, 2 in) shorter than desired length. At this point it is important to end on either line 7 (9, 11) or 12 (16, 20) of chart for the size you are making.

TOE

Set-up round: Remove marker indicating end of round, and k to next marker: this marker now indicates beginning of round.
Next round: K to end of round, repositioning sts across needles if necessary, sm.

Decrease Section

Next round (Dec): * K1, skp, k to within 3 sts of next marker, k2tog, k1, sm; rep from * once more; 4 sts dec.
Next round: K to end of round, sm.
These 2 rounds set pattern. Repeat these 2 rounds a further 9 (10, 11) times until 16 (20, 24) sts remain.

FINISHING

Cut yarn leaving a long thread approx 30cm (12in) long. Divide sole and instep sts evenly across two needles, then with RS facing graft remaining sts together.
Darn in all ends.

Soak in lukewarm soapy water, rinse if required then block to size.

1st Size

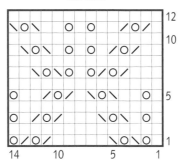

2nd Size

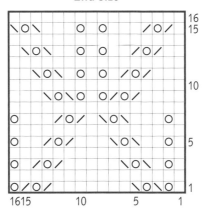

3rd Size

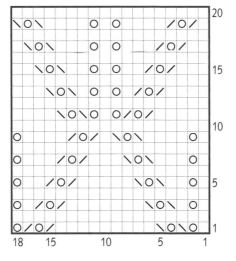

Key

☐	knit
╱	k2tog
╲	skp
⊙	yo
☐	Pattern repeat

1st size only

Round 1: K1, (yo, skp) twice, k5, (k2tog, yo) twice.

Round 2 and all even numbered rounds: K14.

Round 3: K1, yo, k1, skp, yo, skp, k3, k2tog, yo, k2tog, k1, yo.

Round 5: K1, yo, k2, skp, yo, skp, k1, k2tog, yo, k2tog, k2, yo.

Round 7: K3, (k2tog, yo) twice, k1, (yo, skp) twice, k2.

Round 9: K2, k2tog, yo, k2tog, (k1, yo) twice, k1, skp, yo, skp, k1.

Round 11: K1, k2tog, yo, k2tog, k2, yo, k1, yo, k2, skp, yo, skp.

Round 12: K14.

2nd size only

Round 1: K1, (yo, skp) twice, k7, (k2tog, yo) twice.

Round 2 and all even-numbered rounds: K16.

Round 3: K1, yo, k1, skp, yo, skp, k5, k2tog, yo, k2tog, k1, yo.

Round 5: K1, yo, k2, skp, yo, skp, k3, k2tog, yo, k2tog, k2, yo.

Round 7: K1, yo, k3, skp, yo, skp, k1, k2tog, yo, k2tog, k3, yo.

Round 9: K4, (k2tog, yo) twice, k1, (yo, skp) twice, k3.

Round 11: K3, k2tog, yo, k2tog, (k1, yo) twice, k1, skp, yo, skp, k2.

Round 13: K2, k2tog, yo, k2tog, k2, yo, k1, yo, k2, skp, yo, skp, k1.

Round 15: K1, k2tog, yo, k2tog, k3, yo, k1, yo, k3, skp, yo, skp.

Round 16: K16.

3rd size only

Round 1: K1, (yo, skp) twice, k9, (k2tog, yo) twice.

Round 2 and all even numbered rounds: K18.

Round 3: K1, yo, k1, skp, yo, skp, k7, k2tog, yo, k2tog, k1, yo.

Round 5: K1, yo, k2, skp, yo, skp, k5, k2tog, yo, k2tog, k2, yo.

Round 7: K1, yo, k3, skp, yo, skp, k3, k2tog, yo, k2tog, k3, yo.

Round 9: K1, yo, k4, skp, yo, skp, k1, k2tog, yo, k2tog, k4, yo.

Round 11: K5, (k2tog, yo) twice, k1, (yo, skp) twice, k4.

Round 13: K4, k2tog, yo, k2tog, (k1, yo) twice, k1, skp, yo, skp, k3.

Round 15: K3, k2tog, yo, k2tog, k2, yo, k1, yo, k2, skp, yo, skp, k2.

Round 17: K2, k2tog, yo, k2tog, k3, yo, k1, yo, k3, skp, yo, skp, k1.

Round 19: K1, k2tog, yo, k2tog, k4, yo, k1, yo, k4, skp, yo, skp.

Round 20: K18.

···· EVOLUTION ····

Rosa

Rosa is a stylish yoked sweater with a stunning rose motif repeated across the yoke. Rosa is inspired by the Rose Cardigan from The Vintage Shetland Project, which featured a rose motif repeating around the cardigan in bands, first of red then of pink. On some rounds three colours had to be worked to create this beautiful motif with the pattern repeating over the entire garment. I decided to use this motif but simplify it slightly so that only two colours are ever worked on any one round and placed the motifs in a traditional yoke setting with decreases placed between the motifs.

Rosa is also inspired by Floribunda from the Evolution collection itself. After completing Floribunda I couldn't stop thinking about a sweater version of this gorgeous cardigan. Around the farm, sweaters are my go-to. Easy to throw on – not even any buttons to fasten – warm and functional; can be worn with trousers, skirt, shorts or over a dress. So very versatile and also extremely attractive with the decorative floral yoke as used in Floribunda.

Rosa is knitted in Barn, a DK weight yarn, spun from a blend of Jacob and Shetland fleeces, creating a light natural grey shade. It is knitted from the bottom up in the round, commencing with a twisted rib; the body is then worked simply with every round knitted. On reaching the underarm the work is set aside and the sleeves also knitted in the round. The three pieces are then all joined together. Shaping is worked at this point creating attractive 'fully-fashioned' detailing at the armholes. Short rows are worked across the back of the sweater to ensure the neck fits well and then the yoke is worked, using three gorgeous shades of Barn, hand dyed in true 'rose-like' shades. The sweater is designed to have a slightly loose, comfortable fit, but the underarm shaping ensures that the yoke fits neatly on the shoulders.

Rosa is designed to be worn with 10–15cm (4–6in) of positive ease. All charts are read from right to left on every round.

Rosa

YARN

Susan Crawford Barn

100% British wool, a unique blend of Jacob, white Shetland and black Shetland fleeces,

DK weight (225m / 246yds per 100g skein approx)

4 (4, 5, 5, 6, 7, 7, 8, 8) skeins, shade Dry Stone Wall – Yarn A

1 skein, shade Rosehip – Yarn B

1 skein, shade Rosa – Yarn C

1 skein, shade Frond – Yarn D

Yarn kits available from susancrawfordvintage.com

GAUGE

20 sts and 26 rounds = 10cm (4in) over stocking stitch and stranded colourwork worked in the round.

We obtained this gauge using 4mm needles.

If necessary use an alternative needle size to obtain the correct gauge.

SUGGESTED NEEDLES

Small needles: 3.5mm (US 4) circular needle (80–100cm in length)

Set of 3.5mm (US 4) DPNs

Large needles: 4mm (US 6) circular needle (40cm in length)

4mm (US 6) circular needle (80–100cm in length)

Set of 4mm (US 6) DPNs

NOTIONS

Waste yarn or stitch holders

Stitch markers

SAMPLE SHOWN

Rosa is modelled by Susan who is wearing the 4th size with 15cm (6in) of ease.

SIZING AND FINISHING GUIDE

Choose the 'To fit' size closest to your actual chest measurement when deciding which size to knit, bearing in mind the fit you would like to achieve. Use in conjunction with the Schematic to identify which size you should knit.

The measurements given represent the dimensions of the knitting after finishing and blocking according to the pattern instructions and will help you identify which size you should knit. They can also be used to help make adjustments to the finished size of your knitting if needed. The Schematic and the measurements should be used to assist in the pinning-out process to ensure the finished piece is the correct size. Measurements are given in centimetres with inches shown in parentheses.

		1st Size	2nd Size	3rd Size	4th Size	5th Size	6th Size	7th Size	8th Size	9th Size
To fit chest		71–76 (28–30)	81–86 (32–34)	91–97 (36–38)	102–107 (40–42)	112–117 (44–46)	122–127 (48–50)	132–137 (52–54)	142–147 (56–58)	152–157 (60–62)
Finished Measurements										
a	Chest circumference	86 (34½)	96 (38½)	106 (42½)	116 (46½)	126 (50½)	136 (54½)	146 (58½)	156 (62½)	166 (66½)
b	Length to underarm	27½ (11)	29 (11½)	29 (11½)	29½ (11¾)	30½ (12¼)	30½ (12¼)	31½ (12½)	31½ (12½)	32½ (13)
c	Yoke depth	19 (7½)	19½ (7¾)	21 (8½)	21½ (8¾)	24 (9½)	26 (10½)	27½ (11)	28 (11¼)	30 (12)
d	Finished length	46½ (18½)	48½ (19¼)	50 (20)	51 (20½)	54½ (21¾)	56½ (22¾)	59 (23½)	59½ (23¾)	61½ (25)
g	Neck circumference	55 (22)	55 (22)	60 (24)	65 (26)	70 (28)	70 (28)	75 (30)	80 (32)	80 (32)
h	Sleeve length	43 (17¼)	43 (17¼)	44 (17½)	44 (17½)	45 (18)	45 (18)	46 (18½)	46 (18½)	47 (19)
m	Upper arm circumference	30 (12)	32 (12¾)	35 (14)	37 (14¾)	40 (16)	43 (17¼)	46 (18½)	49 (19½)	52 (20¾)

SCHEMATIC

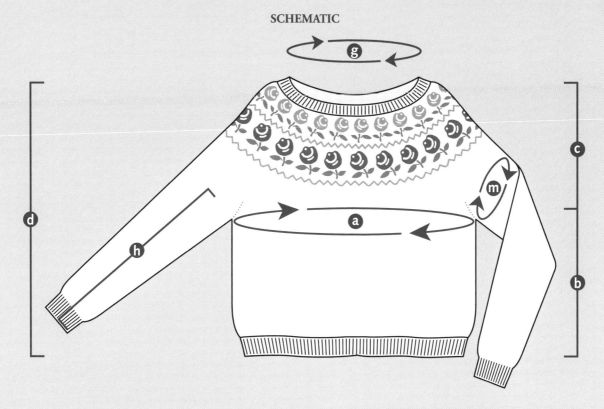

Rosa

DIRECTIONS

BODY

Using smaller circular needle (80–100cm) and yarn A, cast on 172 (192, 212, 232, 252, 272, 292, 312, 332) sts using long tail cast-on method, placing marker after 86 (96, 106, 116, 126, 136, 146, 156, 166) sts to indicate side seam. Join into a round, taking care not to twist sts, and place marker to indicate beginning of round.

Welt

Next round: * K1tbl, p1; rep from * to end of round. Repeat this round until ribbing measures 3cm (1¼in).

Lower Body

Change to larger circular needle (80–100cm). Commence working in stocking stitch (knit every round). Continue as set until work measures 27½ (29, 29, 29½, 30½, 30½, 31½, 31½, 32½) cm (11, 11½, 11½, 11¾, 12¼, 12¼, 12½, 12½, 13 in), or desired length, from cast-on edge.

Armhole divide

Next round (Dec): * K to 3 (4, 4, 5, 5, 6, 6, 7, 7) sts beyond marker, place last 6 (8, 8, 10, 10, 12, 12, 14, 14) sts worked onto waste yarn, removing marker; rep from * once more. Break yarn; 12 (16, 16, 20, 20, 24, 24, 28, 28) sts dec, 160 (176, 196, 212, 232, 248, 268, 284, 304) sts.
Yours sts will now be divided as follows: 80 (88, 98, 106, 116, 124, 134, 142, 152) sts each on front and back.

SLEEVES

Using smaller DPNs and yarn A, cast on 44 (44, 48, 48, 52, 52, 56, 56, 60) sts using long tail cast-on method. Join into a round taking care not to twist sts, placing a marker to indicate beginning of round.

Cuff

Next round: * K1tbl, p1; rep from * to end of round. Repeat this round until cuff measures 5cm (2in) from cast-on edge.
Change to larger DPNs.

Next round (Inc): K1, m1, k to 1 st before marker, m1, k1; 2 sts inc, 46 (46, 50, 50, 54, 54, 58, 58, 62) sts.
K 12 (9, 8, 7, 6, 5, 5, 4, 4) rounds.
Next round (Inc): K1, m1, k to 1 st before marker, m1, k1; 2 sts inc.
Repeat last 13 (10, 9, 8, 7, 6, 6, 5, 5) rounds a further 6 (8, 9, 11, 12, 15, 16, 19, 20) times; 60 (64, 70, 74, 80, 86, 92, 98, 104) sts. Change to larger circular needle (40cm) when needed.

Work with further shaping until sleeve measures 43 (43, 44, 44, 45, 45, 46, 46, 47) cm (17¼, 17¼, 17½, 17½, 18, 18, 18½, 18½, 19 in) from cast-on edge.

Armhole Divide

Without working, move sts around on needle, placing last 3 (4, 4, 5, 5, 6, 6, 7, 7) sts before marker and first 3 (4, 4, 5, 5, 6, 6, 7, 7) sts after marker onto waste yarn, removing marker. Break yarn; 54 (56, 62, 64, 70, 74, 80, 84, 90) sts.

JOIN YOKE

Using larger circular needle (80–100cm) attach yarn A immediately after back sts, pm, then k across 54 (56, 62, 64, 70, 74, 80, 84, 90) sts on first sleeve, pm, k across 80 (88, 98, 106, 116, 124, 134, 142) sts on front, pm, k across 54 (56, 62, 64, 70, 74, 80, 84, 90) sts on second sleeve, pm, k across 40 (44, 49, 53, 58, 62, 67, 71, 76) sts on back and pm to indicated new end of round, k across remaining 40 (44, 49, 53, 58, 62, 67, 71, 76) sts on back. Then break yarn and rearrange stitches to start work after new end of round position, reattach yarn A; 268 (288, 320, 340, 372, 396, 428, 452, 484) sts.

Next round: K to end of round.
Next round (Dec): * K to 3 sts before marker, skp, k1, sm, k1, k2tog; rep from * a further 3 times, k to end of round; 8 sts dec.
Repeat this round a further 6 (5, 9, 9, 9, 9, 10, 13, 14) times; 212 (240, 240, 260, 292, 316, 340, 340, 364) sts.

Your sts will now be divided as follows: 40 (44, 42, 44, 50, 54, 58, 56, 60) sts for each sleeve, and 66 (76, 78, 86, 96, 104, 112, 114, 122) sts for front and back.

1st and 6th sizes only

Next round (Dec): K1, k2tog, k to 3 sts before marker (left back), skp, k1, sm, * k to marker, sm; rep from * a further 2 times, then k1, k2tog, k to last 3 sts, skp, k1; 4 sts dec, 208 (312) sts.

2nd, 3rd and 5th sizes only

Next round (Dec): K1, k2tog, k to 3 sts before marker (left back), skp, k1, sm, k1, k2tog, * k to marker, sm; rep from * once more, then k to 3 sts before marker (right back), skp, k1, sm, k1, k2tog, k to last 3 sts, skp, k1; 6 sts dec, 234 (234, 286) sts.

Next round (Dec): K1, (k2tog), k to last 3 sts, (k2tog), k1;
2 sts dec, 338 (338) sts.

All sizes
K 0 (2, 2, 4, 10, 14, 17, 16, 21) rounds without further
shaping; 208 (234, 234, 260, 286, 312, 338, 338, 364) sts.

SHORT ROW SECTION
Next row (RS): K to 8 sts after left front marker, w&t.
Next row (WS): P to 8 sts after right front marker, w&t.
Next row: K to 6 (6, 6, 6, 7, 7, 8, 8, 9) sts before last turn,
w&t.
Next row: P to 6 (6, 6, 6, 7, 7, 8, 8, 9) sts before last turn,
w&t.
Repeat last 2 rows twice more, knitting back to beginning of
round marker after last turn.
Next round: K to end, reconciling w&ts and removing
additional markers as you work – leaving end of round
marker in place.

Place Yoke Chart
Ensuring you work correct chart for the size you are making,
commence with line 1 of Yoke Chart. On Chart lines 1–3
and 21–23, work the 4-stitch peerie motif repeat 52 (57,
57, 65, 70, 78, 83, 83, 91) times across round (and for 2nd,
3rd, 5th, 7th and 8th sizes only, start peerie rounds with
stitches 1–3 and end rounds with stitches 8–10). For rest of
Chart, work marked 13-stitch, 11-stitch and 7-stitch repeats
16 (18, 18, 20, 22, 24, 26, 26, 28) times across round.

Continue in this manner until all 40 lines of Yoke Chart have
been completed.

You will work decreases on line 24 to give 176 (198, 198,
220, 242, 264, 286, 286, 308) sts and on line 40 to give
112 (126, 126, 140, 154, 168, 182, 182, 196) sts.
Yoke Chart is now complete.

1st size only
Next round (Dec): Using yarn A, K1, k2tog, k to last 3 sts,
k2tog, k1; 2 sts dec, 110 sts.

3rd, 4th, 5th and 6th sizes only
Next round (Dec): Using yarn A, * k 19 (12, 9, 4), k2tog;
rep from * to end of round; 6 (10, 14, 28) sts dec,
120 (130, 140, 140) sts.

2nd, 7th, 8th and 9th sizes only
Next round (Dec): Using yarn A, k 7 (11, 3, 8), * k2tog,
k 5 (3, 6, 3); rep from * to last 7 (11, 3, 8) sts, k to end of
round; 16 (32, 22, 36) sts dec, 110 (150, 160, 160) sts.

All Sizes
Neck Band
Change to smaller circular needle.
Next round: * K1tbl, p1; rep from * to end of round.
Repeat this round until neck band measures 2cm (¾in).
Cast off in k1, p1 rib.

FINISHING
Graft together the 2 sets of 6 (8, 8, 10, 10, 12, 12, 14, 14)
sts held on waste yarn at each underarm.
Soak sweater in lukewarm soapy water, rinse if required,
then pin out to size and leave to dry flat.
Darn in any ends.

1st, 4th, 6th & 9th Sizes

Yoke Chart

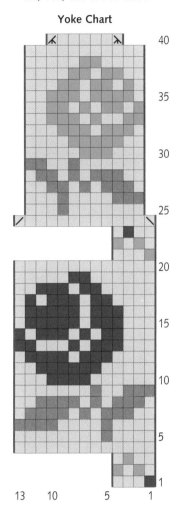

2nd, 3rd, 5th, 7th & 8th Sizes

Yoke Chart

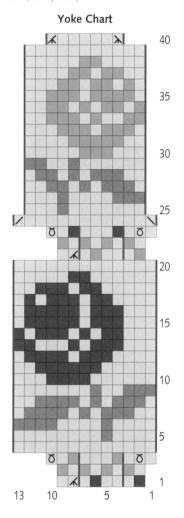

Key

- ⬜ Yarn A (Dry Stone Wall)
- ⬛ Yarn B (Rosehip)
- ⬛ Yarn C (Rosa)
- ⬛ Yarn D (Frond)
- ╱ k2tog
- ╲ skp
- ⷮ k3tog
- ⅄ sk2p
- ℧ m1
- ⬜ Pattern repeat

···· EVOLUTION ····

Steek

Steek was inspired by Tait, a uniquely constructed beret, which I recreated for The Vintage Shetland Project. Like Tait, Steek is constructed in a highly unusual way, knitted partly vertically and partly horizontally, creating a powerful visual effect. It is also inspired, as its name suggests, by steeks and in particular, by the many steek charts created for The Vintage Shetland Project: each one creates a bold, graphic pattern in its own right, which is usually largely ignored other than to serve as a bridge from one part of a garment to another. This design instead celebrates the beauty of those steek charts.

Steek is knitted using Byre, a fingering weight, worsted-spun wool, spun from a blend of Jacob and Shetland fleeces to create a natural shade of soft grey. The beautiful, hand-dyed autumnal colours combined with this are inspired by the farming landscape which surrounds me.

Steek is knitted sideways, casting on stitches for its height rather than its circumference. The hat begins with a provisional cast-on. Rows of stranded colourwork make up each of the panels with crown shaping created by short row shaping. Although only two colours are used in any one row, the construction creates the illusion of multiple colours in each row. An unusual and innovative construction which creates a fascinating surface pattern and an intriguing knit!

The pattern chart shows one panel of the hat and begins with a wrong side row. The chart is then worked back and forth with purl rows worked on the wrong side. The hat builds by the repetition of this panel until the correct number of panels have been knitted for the size needed. As the hat is knitted flat charts are read from right to left on right side, knit rows and from left to right on wrong side, purl rows.

Steek

YARN

Susan Crawford Byre

100% British wool, a unique blend of Jacob, white Shetland and black Shetland fleeces,

4 Ply weight (100m / 109yds per 25g skein approx)

1 skein, shade Dry Stone Wall – Yarn A

1 skein, shade Loam – Yarn B

1 skein, shade Gate Post – Yarn C

1 skein, shade Clay – Yarn D

1 skein, shade Rusty Tractor – Yarn E

Yarn kits available from susancrawfordvintage.com

GAUGE

30 sts & 34 rows = 10cm (4in) measured over stranded colourwork worked flat, after blocking.

We obtained this gauge using 3mm needles.

If necessary use an alternative needle size to obtain the correct gauge.

SUGGESTED NEEDLES

Small needles: 2.75mm (US 2) circular needle (80cm in length)

Large needles: 3mm (US 3) circular (80–100cm in length) needle or 1 pair of 3mm (US 3) straight needles

Crochet hook: 3.5mm (US E) hook

NOTIONS

Waste yarn

Removable stitch marker

Button

SAMPLE SHOWN

Steek is modelled by Susan who is wearing the 3rd size and has a 50cm (20in) head circumference.

SIZING AND FINISHING GUIDE

The measurements given represent the dimensions of the knitting after finishing and blocking according to the pattern instructions. The schematic and the measurements should be used to assist in the blocking process to ensure the finished piece is the correct size. Measurements are given in centimetres with inches shown in parentheses.

	1st	2nd	3rd	4th	5th
To fit head circumference	42½ (17)	46½ (18½)	50 (20)	55 (22)	60 (24)

Finished Measurements

		1st	2nd	3rd	4th	5th
u	Height without brim	20 (8)	20 (8)	20 (8)	20 (8)	20 (8)
w	Height with brim	23½ (9½)	23½ (9½)	23½ (9½)	23½ (9½)	23½ (9½)
x	Circumference at widest point	49½ (19¾)	49½ (19¾)	57½ (23)	57½ (23)	66 (26½)
y	Circumference at brim	37½ (15)	42½ (17)	47 (18¾)	50 (20)	55 (22)

SCHEMATIC

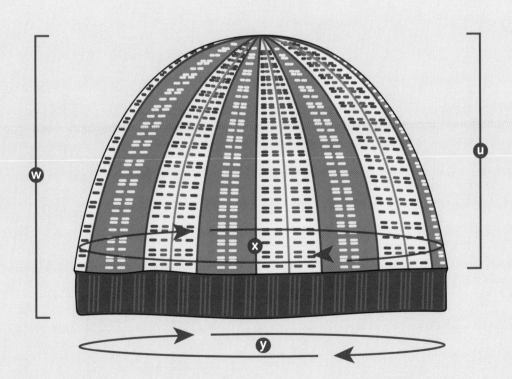

DIRECTIONS

PROVISIONAL CAST-ON

Using the crochet hook and waste yarn, work a chain of approximately 70 sts, pull yarn through final loop and place a removable marker in the same loop.

Row 1 (WS): Using larger needles and yarn D, pick up and purl one st into bar at back of each crochet chain until 60 sts worked.

FIRST PANEL

Place Chart

** **Row 2** (RS): Working from line 2 of Chart, k in pattern across 58 sts, w&t.

Row 3 (WS): Working from line 3 of Chart, p in pattern to end of row.

Continue as set by these two rows, working back and forth, working 4 sts less on each subsequent k row until line 13 of Chart completed.

Row 14 (RS): Working from line 14 of Chart, k across all sts, reconciling all w&ts as you reach them.

Row 15 (WS): Working from line 15 of Chart, p to end of row.

Row 16: Working from line 16 of Chart, k 38 sts in pattern, w&t.

Row 17: Working from line 17 of Chart, p in pattern to end of row.

Row 18: Working from line 18 of Chart, k 42 sts in pattern, reconciling previous w&t, then w&t.

Row 19: Working from line 19 of Chart, p in pattern to end of row.

Continue as set by these two rows, working back and forth, working 4 sts more on each subsequent k row and reconciling previous w&t until line 27 of Chart completed.

Row 28 (RS): Working from line 28 of Chart, k to end of row. ***

SUBSEQUENT PANELS

Place Chart

Work 4 (4, 5, 5, 6) further panels as follows:

Row 1 (WS): Working from line 1 of Chart, p in pattern to end of row.

Work as for First Panel from ** to ***.

FINAL PANEL

Place Chart

Row 1 (WS): Working from line 1 of Chart, p in pattern to end of row.

Work as for First Panel from ** to *** but ending with line 27 of Chart.

JOIN PANELS

Commencing at end marked with removable marker, carefully undo provisional cast-on placing live sts from first row worked onto smaller needle. Commencing at lower edge, with WS together and using Yarn B graft live sts on smaller needle to live sts on larger needle. Fasten off, leaving a long tail.

BRIM

Using smaller circular needle and Yarn B, and with RS facing, pick up and k 128 (144, 160, 168, 176) sts evenly around bottom edge of hat, placing a marker to indicate beginning of round.

Next round: * K2, p2; rep from * to end of round.
This round forms pattern. Repeat this round until brim measures 3½cm (1½in). Cast off in rib.

FINISHING

Using long tail left at crown, sew running stitches around opening at crown then draw in tightly taking long tail to WS. Darn in all other ends.

Soak in lukewarm, soapy water, rinse if required. Place over 27½cm (11in) dinner plate or hat form and leave to dry. Using long tail attach button to centre of crown. Darn in any remaining ends.

Chart

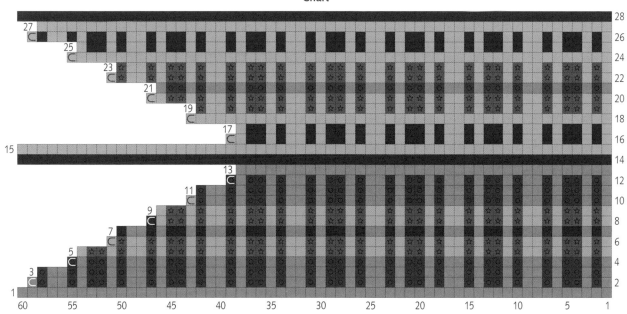

Key

- ▨ Yarn A (Dry Stone Wall)
- ■ Yarn B (Loam)
- ☆ Yarn C (Gate Post)
- ▨ Yarn D (Clay)
- ◉ Yarn E (Rusty Tractor)
- ⊂ w&t

···· EVOLUTION ····

Tavis

Tavis was inspired by its companion-pattern Tait and also by Helen from The Vintage Shetland Project, where both a scarf and a cowl version of this intriguing tubular design were created. Tavis uses a colourwork pattern to match that of Steek so the two can be worn as a set or separately and uses a similar but somewhat simplified construction to Helen.

Commencing with a provisional cast-on, Tavis is a circular, tubular cowl, knitted in the round with alternating bands of colourwork and stocking stitch. The colourwork pattern, like Steek, is inspired by the steek charts used for Hilda in The Vintage Shetland Project. Once the knitting has been completed the cowl is joined together by grafting the final round of live stitches to the first round worked.

Tavis is knitted using Byre, a fingering weight, worsted-spun wool, spun from a blend of Jacob and Shetland fleeces to create a natural shade of soft grey. The beautiful, hand-dyed autumnal colours combined with this are inspired by the farming landscape which surrounds me and are the same as those used for Steek.

Tavis can be knitted in either a long or a short version with the long version long enough to wrap around the neck twice and both versions use the same simple charts which are worked from right to left on every round.

Tavis

YARN

Susan Crawford Byre

100% British wool, a unique blend of Jacob, white Shetland and black Shetland fleeces,

4 Ply weight (400m / 436yds per 100g skein approx)

1 skein, shade Dry Stone Wall – Yarn A

1 skein, shade Loam – Yarn B

1 skein, shade Gate Post – Yarn C

1 skein, shade Clay – Yarn D

1 skein, shade Rusty Tractor – Yarn E

Yarn kits available from susancrawfordvintage.com

GAUGE

27 sts & 37 rounds = 10cm (4in) over stocking stitch and stranded colourwork knitted in the round, after blocking.

We obtained this gauge using 3mm needles.

If necessary use an alternative needle size to obtain the correct gauge.

SUGGESTED NEEDLES

2 × 3mm (US 2/3) circular needles (60cm in length for Shorter cowl, 100cm in length for Longer cowl)

Crochet hook: 3.5mm (US E) hook

NOTIONS

Wasle yarn

Removable stitch marker

SAMPLE SHOWN

Tavis is modelled by Susan who is wearing the longer length cowl.

SIZING AND FINISHING GUIDE

The measurements given represent the dimensions of the knitting after finishing and blocking according to the pattern instructions. The Schematic and the measurements should be used to assist in the pinning-out process to ensure the finished piece is the correct size. Measurements are given in centimetres with inches shown in parentheses.

Finished Measurements

		Short	Long
X	Circumference	83 (33¼)	166 (66½)
W	Height	14 (5½)	18½ (7½)

SCHEMATIC

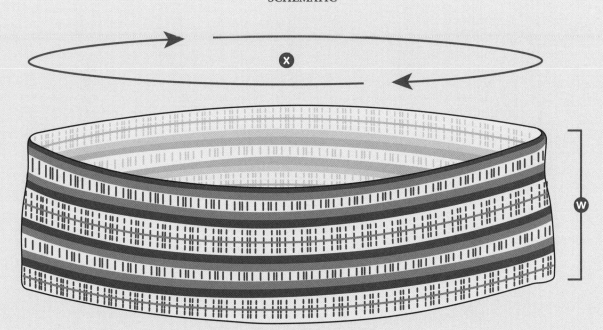

DIRECTIONS

PROVISIONAL CAST-ON

Using a crochet hook and waste yarn, work a chain of approximately 230 (460) sts, placing a removable marker in the final chain.

Next row: Using appropriate needle to obtain gauge (60cm or 100cm depending on cowl circumference), and yarn B, pick up and purl one st into bar at back of each crochet chain until 224 (448) sts worked. Join into a round, placing a marker to indicate beginning of round.

** Place Chart A

Next round: Commencing with line 1 of Chart A, work 8-st pattern rep 28 (56) times across round.
This round sets pattern. Continue working as set until all 13 lines of Chart A have been completed.

Next round: Using yarn B only, k to end of round.
Repeat this round a further 3 times.

Place Chart B

Next round: Commencing with line 1 of Chart B, work 8-st pattern rep 28 (56) times across round.
This round sets pattern. Continue working as set until all 13 lines of Chart B have been completed.

Next round: Using yarn B only, k to end of round.
Repeat this round a further 3 times. ***

Repeat from ** to *** once (twice) more.

Place Chart A

Next round: Commencing with line 1 of Chart A, work 8-st pattern rep 28 (56) times across round.
This round sets pattern. Continue working as set until all 13 lines of Chart A have been completed.

Next round: Using yarn B only, k to end of round.
Repeat this round a further 3 times.

Place Chart B

Next round: Commencing with line 1 of Chart B, work 8-st pattern rep 28 (56) times across round.
This round sets pattern. Continue working as set until all 13 lines of Chart B have been completed.

Next round: Using yarn B only, k to end of round.
Repeat this round once more, leaving sts on needle when final round completed with a long tail attached.

FINISHING

Darn in all ends, leaving long tail.

Commencing at end of provisional cast-on marked with removable marker, carefully undo crochet cast-on placing live sts from first round worked onto a second circular needle. With WS together and using yarn B still attached to final round of cowl worked, graft live sts from first and final rounds together, joining in new lengths of yarn as needed. Ensure all graft stitches are regular before fastening off and drawing yarn end through to inside of cowl.

Soak in lukewarm soapy water, rinse if required. Pin out to size. To ensure even blocking, cut a piece of cardboard to the finished dimensions of the cowl. Cover in plastic or sticky tape and place inside the cowl, then leave the cowl to dry flat.

Chart A

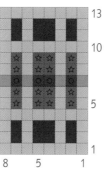

13
10
5
1

8   5   1

Chart B

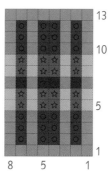

13
10
5
1

8   5   1

Key

- Yarn A (Dry Stone Wall)
- Yarn B (Loam)
- Yarn C (Gate Post)
- Yarn D (Clay)
- Yarn E (Rusty Tractor)
- Pattern repeat

Annemor

Annemor is a easy-to-wear, open front jacket with a relaxed, slightly boxy fit. It was inspired by the interweaving of Shetland and Norwegian knitting cultures as first revealed to me by the legendary Annemor Sundbø, a subject I then explored further in The Vintage Shetland Project.

The attractive colour work edgings of the jacket are inspired by Suffragette from The Vintage Shetland Project which used these bold, graphic motifs to great effect. I have paired these with a traditional Norwegian all-over motif and used a strongly contrasting colourway. The lower body is worked in the round from the bottom up with a steek at centre front. The body is divided at the armholes and two further small steeks added for each armhole. The shoulders are grafted together and then the sleeves are picked up around the armholes and knitted downwards. A small amount of shaping is worked on the sleeves before the coordinating cuffs are knitted. Finally the front steek is cut open and stitches picked up to knit the front band. Small hems are worked on the welt and cuffs to create structure and to ensure the jacket hangs well. A facing is also knitted as part of the front band and this is then sewn in place covering the steek opening.

In order to provide a wide range of sizes two gauge options are provided. It is extremely important to match your gauge to that specified for your chosen size otherwise the jacket will not be the correct size – and I should know! You will see below that Annemor is designed to be worn with approximately 20–27½cm (8–11in) of positive ease. For the sample which I would be wearing for the photographs in the book, I planned to knit the 4th size which with a finished circumference of 117cm (46¾in) around the chest would give me my desired ease of about 20cm (8in). The 4th size has the same stitch count as the 3rd size but the 4th size requires a gauge of 26 sts to every 10cm (4in) whilst the 3rd size requires a gauge of 28 sts. In error I used 3.25mm needles instead of 3.5mm and this has meant my 4th size garment is now actually only the 3rd size. I am lucky, the jacket still fits me; but instead of that slightly loose, oversized look that I wanted, I have a more fitted jacket with only around 7cm (3in) of ease. So take care!

Full colour charts are provided which are read from right to left on every round when working in the round, and when working flat are read from right to left on right side rows, and from left to right on wrong side, purl rows.

Annemor is knitted in Excelana 4 Ply, a standard fingering weight pure wool, using a blend of British breed fleeces from the Exmoor Mule and Bluefaced Leicester sheep, to create a soft, yet sturdy, yarn which is perfect for colourwork. I used three shades of grey from the darkest Charcoal, to Persian Grey and finally Sheffield Steel. To these I added Limestone a cool, pale oatmeal shade.

Annemor is designed to be worn with approximately 20–27½cm (8–11in) of positive ease.

Annemor

YARN

Susan Crawford Excelana 4 Ply, 100% British wool (159m / 174yds per 50g skein)

2 (2, 2, 2, 2, 2, 2, 2, 2, 2, 3, 3) skeins, shade Limestone – Yarn A

1 (1, 1, 1, 1, 1, 2, 2, 2, 2, 2, 2) skeins, shade Persian Grey – Yarn B

6 (7, 7, 8, 8, 9, 9, 10, 10, 11, 12, 12) skeins, shade Charcoal – Yarn C

1 (1, 1, 1, 1, 1, 1, 1, 1, 1, 1, 1) skeins, shade Sheffield Steel – Yarn D

Yarn kits available from susancrawfordvintage.com

GAUGE

1st, 3rd, 5th, 7th and 9th sizes

28 sts & 29 rounds = 10cm (4in) over stranded colourwork knitted in the round and flat, after blocking.

We used a 3.25mm needle to obtain this gauge.

2nd, 4th, 6th, 8th, 10th, 11th and 12th sizes

26 sts & 27 rounds = 10cm (4in) over stranded colourwork knitted in the round and flat, after blocking.

We used a 3.5mm needle to obtain this gauge.

If necessary use an alternative needle size to obtain the correct gauge.

SUGGESTED NEEDLES

1st, 3rd, 5th, 7th and 9th sizes

Small needles: 2.75mm (US 2) circular needle (40cm in length)

2.75mm (US 2) circular needle (80–100cm in length)

Large needles: 3.25mm (US 3) circular needle (40cm in length)

3.25mm (US 3) circular needle (60cm in length)

3.25mm (US 3) circular needle (80–100cm in length)

2nd, 4th, 6th, 8th, 10th, 11th and 12th sizes

Small needles: 2.75mm (US 2) circular needle (40cm in length)

2.75mm (US 2) circular needle (80–100cm in length)

Large needles: 3.5mm (US 4) circular needle (40cm in length)

3.5mm (US 4) circular needle (60cm in length)

3.5mm (US 4) circular needle (80–100cm in length)

NOTIONS

Stitch markers

Waste yarn or stitch holders

Crochet hook of same size as large needles

SAMPLE SHOWN

Annemor is modelled by Susan wearing the 3rd size with approximately 7cm (3in) of ease (please see pattern notes on previous page)

SIZING AND FINISHING GUIDE

Choose the 'To fit' size closest to your actual chest measurement when deciding which size to knit, bearing in mind the fit you would like to achieve. Use in conjunction with the Schematic to identify which size you should knit.

The measurements given represent the dimensions of the knitting after finishing and blocking according to the pattern instructions and will help you identify which size you should knit. They can also be used to help make adjustments to the finished size of your knitting if needed. The Schematic and the measurements should be used to assist in the pinning-out process to ensure the finished piece is the correct size. Measurements are given in centimetres with inches shown in parentheses.

		1st Size	2nd Size	3rd Size	4th Size	5th Size	6th Size	7th Size	8th Size	9th Size	10th Size	11th Size	12th Size
To fit chest		71–76 (28–30)	81 (32)	86–91 (34–36)	97 (38)	101 (40)	107–112 (42–44)	117 (46)	122–127 (48–50)	132 (52)	137–142 (54–56)	147–157 (58–62)	162–167 (64–66)
Finished Measurements													
a	Chest Circumference	95 (38)	103 (41¼)	108 (43¼)	117 (46¾)	120½ (48¼)	131 (52½)	133½ (53½)	144½ (57¾)	146½ (58½)	158½ (63½)	170 (68)	186 (74½)
b	Length to underarm	34 (13½)	35 (14)	37 (14¾)	38 (15¼)	39½ (15¾)	39½ (15¾)	39½ (15¾)	39½ (15¾)	41 (16½)	41 (16½)	41 (16½)	41 (16½)
c	Armhole Depth	19 (7½)	19 (7½)	19 (7½)	19 (7½)	20½ (8¼)	22 (8¾)	22 (8¾)	23½ (9½)	23 (9¼)	25 (10)	28 (11)	28 (11)
d	Finished length	53 (21¼)	54 (21½)	56 (22½)	57 (22¾)	60 (24)	61½ (24½)	61½ (24½)	63 (25¼)	64 (25½)	66 (26½)	69 (26¾)	69 (27½)
e	Cross back	43 (17¼)	49 (19)	47½ (19¾)	54 (21¾)	56 (22½)	61 (24½)	62½ (25)	68 (27¼)	69 (27½)	75 (30)	82 (32¾)	89 (35½)
h	Sleeve length	42½ (17)	41 (16½)	42½ (17)	41 (16½)	42½ (17)	41 (16½)	42½ (17)	41 (16½)	42½ (17)	41 (16½)	41 (16½)	41 (16½)
m	Upper arm circumference	41 (16½)	44 (17½)	43 (17¼)	46 (18½)	45 (18)	48½ (19½)	49½ (19¾)	53 (21¼)	51½ (20½)	55½ (22¼)	57½ (23)	57½ (23)

SCHEMATIC

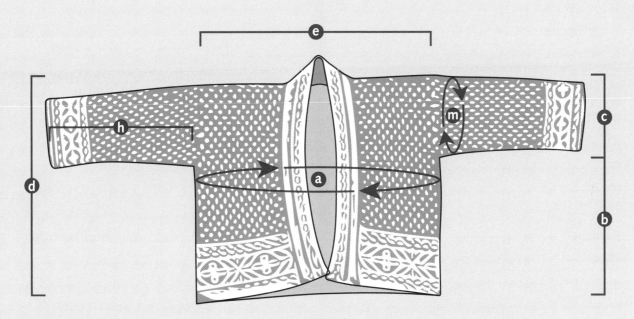

BODY

Welt
Using smaller circular needle (80–100cm) and yarn C, cast on 217 (217, 253, 253, 289, 289, 325, 325, 361, 361, 397, 433) sts.

Ribbing
Next row (RS): * K1tbl, p1; rep from * to last st, k1tbl.
Next row (WS): * P1tbl, k1; rep from * to last st, p1tbl.
Repeat these two rows once more.

Steek Placement
Next round: Using cable cast-on method and yarn C, cast on 6 sts, pm, k to end of row, pm, then join work into a round by moving first 3 sts on left needle tip onto right needle tip, pm to indicate new beginning of round. Break yarn C; 223 (223, 259, 259, 295, 295, 331, 331, 367, 367, 403, 439) sts, including 6 steek sts.

Change to larger circular needle (80–100cm) and join yarn A to first stitch after beginning of round marker.
Next round: Using yarn A only, k to end of round.

Chart Placement
Next round: Commencing with line 1, work sts 4–6 of Steek Chart A across first 3 sts on needle, sm, then commencing with line 1 of Chart A, work 36 sts of marked patt rep 6 (6, 7, 7, 8, 8, 9, 9, 10, 10, 11, 12) times, then work st 37 once only, sm, then work sts 1–3 of Steek Chart A.
This round sets pattern. Continue working in this manner until all 40 lines of Chart A and Steek Chart A have been completed.

Next round (Inc): Using yarn C only, k4, m1, k 72 (72, 84, 84, 96, 96, 108, 108, 120, 120, 132, 144), m1, k 71 (71, 83, 83, 95, 95, 107, 107, 119, 119, 131, 143), m1, k 72 (72, 84, 84, 96, 96, 108, 108, 120, 120, 132, 144), m1, k4; 227 (227, 263, 263, 299, 299, 335, 335, 371, 371, 407, 443) sts, including 6 steek sts.

Chart Placement
1st, 3rd, 5th, 6th, 7th and 8th sizes only
Next round: Commencing with line 1, work sts 4–6 of Steek Chart B, sm, commencing with line 1 of Chart B, work st 1, then work 6-st patt rep 36 (42, 48, 48, 54, 54) times across round, then work sts 8–11, sm, finally work sts 1–3 of Steek Chart B.

This round sets pattern. Continue working in this manner until all 8 lines of Chart B and Steek Chart B have been completed. Repeat a further 6 (7, 8, 7, 8, 7) times, placing side seam markers on final round as follows: Starting at beginning of round, patt 47 (56, 65, 64, 74, 73) sts, pm, patt 133 (151, 169, 171, 187, 189) sts, pm, patt 47 (56, 65, 64, 74, 73) sts.

2nd, 4th, 9th, 10th, 11th and 12th sizes only
Next round: Commencing with line 1, work sts 4–6 of Steek Chart B, sm, then commencing with line 1 of Chart B, work st 1 then work 6-st patt rep 36 (42, 60, 60, 66, 72) times across round, then work sts 8–11, sm, finally work sts 1–3 of Steek Chart B.

This round sets pattern. Continue working in this manner until all 8 lines of Chart B and Steek Chart B have been completed. Repeat a further 5 (6, 8, 7, 7, 7) times, then repeat lines 1–4 only once more, placing side seam markers on final round as follows: Starting at beginning of round, patt 46 (55, 83, 82, 91, 100) sts, pm, patt 135 (153, 205, 207, 225, 243) sts, pm, patt 46 (55, 83, 82, 91, 100) sts.

All sizes
Shape Armholes and Insert Armhole Steeks
Set-up round: Maintaining patt as set, * patt to 6 sts before side seam marker, place next 12 sts unworked onto waste yarn, pm, and cast on 4 sts using backward loop method as follows: yarn A, yarn B, yarn B, yarn A, pm; rep from * once more, patt to end of round; 211 (211, 247, 247, 283, 283, 319, 319, 355, 355, 391, 427) sts. Your sts should be arranged as follows; 3 steek sts, 38 (37, 47, 46, 56, 55, 65, 64, 74, 73, 82, 91) sts for right front, 4 steek sts for armhole, 121 (123, 139, 141, 157, 159, 175, 177, 193, 195, 213, 231) sts for back, 4 steek sts, 38 (37, 47, 46, 56, 55, 65, 64, 74, 73, 82, 91) sts for left front, 3 steek sts.

Next round: Maintaining patt as set, * work to side seam marker, work line 2 (6, 2, 6, 2, 2, 2, 2, 6, 6, 6, 6) of Armhole Steek Chart across next 4 sts, sm; rep from * once more, then work to end of round.
This round sets pattern. Continue in this manner until a total of 54 (50, 54, 50, 58, 58, 62, 62, 66, 66, 74, 74) rounds have been completed, including set-up round and ending with line 2 or 6 of Chart B and Steek Charts.

Next round (Dec): Maintaining patt as set, * work to side seam marker, cast off 4 steek sts; rep from * once more, work to steek marker, cast off 6 steek sts; 14 sts dec.

Join Shoulders

Distribute front and back sts evenly across 2 circular needles. With front of work facing and using yarn C, graft 38 (37, 47, 46, 56, 55, 65, 64, 74, 73, 82, 91) sts of left front to corresponding sts on back. Turn work so that back of work is now facing and using yarn C, graft first 38 (37, 47, 46, 56, 55, 65, 64, 74, 73, 82, 91) sts of back to corresponding sts on right front. Place remaining 45 (49, 45, 49, 45, 49, 45, 49, 45, 49, 49, 49) sts for back neck onto waste yarn.

SLEEVES

Reinforce armhole steeks and cut open.

Place 12 sts held on waste yarn onto smaller circular needle (40cm), then place first 6 sts back onto waste yarn. Using yarn C and larger circular needle (60cm), k 6 sts from smaller circular needle, then pick up and k 51 (51, 54, 54, 57, 57, 63, 63, 66, 66, 69, 69) sts up one side of armhole, then pick up and k 51 (51, 54, 54, 57, 57, 63, 63, 66, 66, 69, 69) sts down remaining side of armhole, then k remaining 6 sts held on waste yarn; 114 (114, 120, 120, 126, 126, 138, 138, 144, 144, 150, 150) sts. Place marker to indicate beginning of round.

Place Chart

Set-up round: Commencing with line 1 of Chart B, work 6-st pattern repeat only 19 (19, 20, 20, 21, 21, 23, 23, 24, 24, 25, 25) times across round.
This round sets pattern.

Sleeve Shaping

Maintaining pattern as set, commence decreasing as follows:
Work without shaping for a further 9 (8, 6, 5, 5, 4, 9, 8, 6, 5, 4, 4) rounds.
Next round (Dec): Maintaining patt, k1, skp, patt to last 3 sts before marker, k2tog, k1; 2 sts dec.

Repeat last 10 (9, 7, 6, 6, 5, 10, 9, 7, 6, 5, 5) rounds a further 8 (8, 11, 11, 14, 14, 8, 8, 11, 11, 14, 14) times, changing to larger circular needle (40cm) when needed; a further 16 (16, 22, 22, 28. 28, 16, 16, 22, 22, 28, 28) sts dec, 96 (96, 96, 96, 96, 96, 120, 120, 120, 120, 120, 120) sts.

Continue without further shaping for a further 6 (3, 12, 12, 6, 9, 6, 3, 12, 12, 9, 9) rounds ending with line 4 or 8 of Chart B.

Cuff

Commencing with line 1 of Chart C work 24-st pattern repeat 4 (4, 4, 4, 4, 4, 5, 5, 5, 5, 5, 5) times across round. Continue in this manner until all 27 lines of Chart C have been completed.

Change to yarn C and smaller circular needle (40cm).
Next round: K to end of round.
Next round: * K1tbl, p1; rep from * to end of round. Repeat this round three more times. Cast off.

HEMS

Welt

Turn work to WS and using yarn C turn 4 rounds of single rib on welt to WS and slip stitch into place.

Cuffs

Turn sleeves to WS and using yarn C turn 4 rounds of single rib on cuff to WS and slip stitch into place.

Centre Front Steek

Turn work to RS and reinforce steek. Cut down length of steek.

Front Band and Facing
1st, 3rd, 5th, 7th and 9th sizes only

Commencing at lower edge of right front, with RS facing and using yarn C and smaller circular needle (80–100cm), pick up and k 120 (120, 120, 132, 132) sts up right front, then k1, m1, k14, m1, k15, m1, k14, m1, k1, across 45 sts held on waste yarn at back neck, then pick up and k 120 (120, 120, 132, 132) sts down left front; 289 (289, 289, 313, 313) sts.

2nd, 4th, 6th, 8th, 10th, 11th and 12th sizes only

Commencing at lower edge of right front, with RS facing and using yarn C and smaller circular needle (80–100cm), pick up and k 120 (120, 120, 132, 132, 144, 144) sts up right front, then k across 49 sts held on waste yarn at back neck, then pick up and k 120 (120, 120, 132, 132, 144, 144) sts down left front; (289, 289, 289, 313, 313, 337, 337) sts.

All sizes
Change to larger circular needle (80–100cm).

Place Chart
Next row (WS): Using yarn C, p to end of row.
Next row (RS): Commencing with line 1 of Chart D, work
6-st patt rep 48 (48, 48, 48, 48, 48, 52, 52, 52, 52, 56, 56)
times across row, then work st 7 once.
Next row (WS): Commencing with line 2 of Chart D and
purling each st, work st 7 once, then work 6-st patt rep 48
(48, 48, 48, 48, 48, 52, 52, 52, 52, 56, 56) times across
row.

These two rows set pattern. Continue in this manner until all
22 lines of Chart D have been completed.
Change to smaller circular needle (80–100cm) and yarn C.
Next round: K to end of round.
Next round: Using yarn C, * k1, p1; rep from * to end of
row.

Repeat this row until ribbing measures same depth as band.
Cast off in rib leaving a long tail. Turn single rib to WS and
slip stitch into place across line of picked up stitches.

Using appropriately sized crochet hook and yarn C, work a
row of double crochet (or single crochet if used to US
terminology) across bottom edge of front bands, working
each stitch through both layers of front band and facing.
Fasten off.

FINISHING
Darn in all ends. Soak in lukewarm soapy water, rinse if
required then pin out to size and leave to dry flat.

Steek A

Chart A

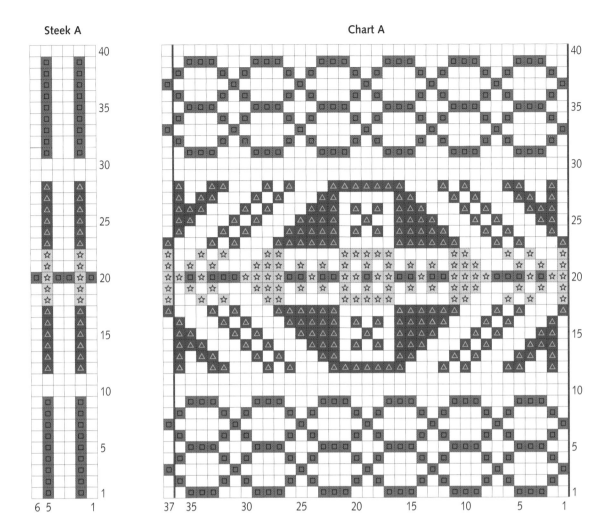

Chart B   **Steek B**   **Armhole Steek**

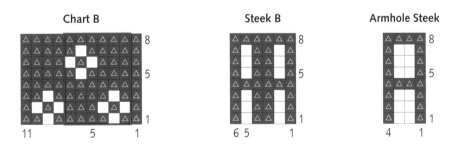

Key

☐ Yarn A (Limestone)

▣ Yarn B (Persian Grey)

△ Yarn C (Charcoal)

☆ Yarn D (Sheffield Steel)

☐ Pattern repeat

Chart C

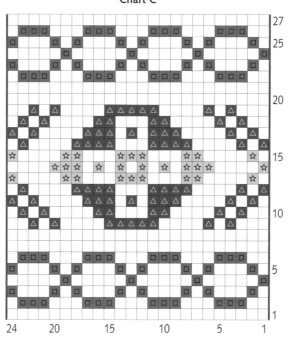

Chart D

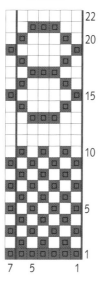

Key

- ☐ Yarn A (Limestone)
- ▣ Yarn B (Persian Grey)
- △ Yarn C (Charcoal)
- ☆ Yarn D (Sheffield Steel)
- ☐ Pattern repeat

···· EVOLUTION ····

Maggy

Maggy uses the simple, geometric recurring motifs found in Margaret, from The Vintage Shetland Project. To facilitate the easy lengthening – or shortening – of the waistcoat I have used the same motifs throughout, making it simple to add additional motifs where needed. Rather than creating another cardigan I loved the option of a colourwork waistcoat, providing warmth were most needed but with easy to remove if the temperature increases. The bands and welt are knitted in moss (seed) stitch echoing the finishing touches found on Vaila and creating a neat, stylish edge. Buttons are added for decoration over press fasteners, and be attached to either button band.

Maggy is knitted using Byre, a fingering weight, worsted-spun wool, spun from a blend of Jacob and Shetland fleeces to create a natural shade of soft grey. The beautiful, hand-dyed autumnal colours combined with this are inspired by the landscape which surrounds me.

Three body lengths are included in the pattern, simple choose whether to knit the short, medium or long length; however to adjust the length to your exact preference, determine the number of extra rounds required and add additional patterning at the start of the body, leaving patterning unchanged at the underarm and above. Allow the following amounts of yarn for each additional pattern repeat worked:

Yarn A – approx 25g
Yarn B – approx 10g (plus an additional 15g for added length in front bands)
Yarn C – approx 10g
Yarn D – approx 25g
Yarn E – approx 10g

If you have adjusted the length to your personal preference remember to add or remove stitches when working front bands at a rate of 3 stitches for every 4 rounds worked.

Individual charts are provided for each size with accompanying Steek charts as needed ensuring the pattern is easy to follow and pleasurable to knit. All charts are read from right to left on every round. Maggy is designed to be worn with approximately 2½–10cm (1–4in) of positive ease.

Maggy

YARN

Susan Crawford Byre

100% British wool, a unique blend of Jacob, white Shetland and black Shetland fleeces,

4 Ply weight (400m / 436yds per 100g skein approx)

Short Length

1 (1, 1, 1, 1, 2, 2, 2, 2, 2, 2) skeins, shade Dry Stone Wall – Yarn A

1 (1, 1, 1, 1, 2, 2, 2, 2, 2, 2) skeins, shade Undergrowth – Yarn B

1 (1, 1, 1, 1, 1, 1, 1, 1, 1) skeins, shade Moss Covered Wall – Yarn C

1 (1, 1, 1, 1, 1, 1, 1, 1, 1) skeins, shade Berry Picking – Yarn D

1 (1, 1, 1, 1, 1, 1, 1, 1, 1) skeins, shade Hay Bale – Yarn E

Medium Length

1 (1, 2, 2, 2, 2, 2, 2, 2, 2) skeins, shade Dry Stone Wall – Yarn A

1 (1, 1, 2, 2, 2, 2, 2, 2, 2) skeins, shade Undergrowth – Yarn B

1 (1, 1, 1, 1, 1, 1, 1, 1, 1) skeins, shade Moss Covered Wall – Yarn C

1 (1, 1, 1, 1, 1, 1, 1, 1, 2) skeins, shade Berry Picking – Yarn D

1 (1, 1, 1, 1, 1, 1, 1, 1, 1) skeins, shade Hay Bale – Yarn E

Long Length

2 (2, 2, 2, 2, 2, 2, 2, 2, 2) skeins, shade Dry Stone Wall – Yarn A

2 (2, 2, 2, 2, 2, 2, 2, 2, 2) skeins, shade Undergrowth – Yarn B

1 (1, 1, 1, 1, 1, 1, 1, 1, 1) skeins, shade Moss Covered Wall – Yarn C

1 (1, 1, 1, 1, 1, 2, 2, 2, 2) skeins, shade Berry Picking – Yarn D

1 (1, 1, 1, 1, 1, 1, 1, 1, 1) skeins, shade Hay Bale – Yarn E

Yarn kits available from susancrawfordvintage.com

GAUGE

28 sts and 30 rounds = 10cm (4in) over stranded colourwork knitted in the round.

We obtained this gauge using 3.25mm needles.

If necessary use an alternative needle size to obtain the correct gauge.

SUGGESTED NEEDLES

Small needles: 2.75mm (US 2) circular needle (40–60cm in length)

2.75mm (US 2) circular needle (80–100cm in length)

Large needles: 3.25mm (US 3) circular needle (80–100cm in length)

NOTIONS

Waste yarn or stitch holders · Stitch markers · 5 (6, 7) buttons & press fastenings · Matching thread · Sewing needle

SAMPLE SHOWN

Maggy is modelled by Susan wearing the 5th size, short length with 9cm (3.5in) of ease.

SIZING AND FINISHING GUIDE

Choose the 'To fit' size closest to your actual chest measurement when deciding which size to knit, bearing in mind the fit you would like to achieve. Use in conjunction with the Schematic to identify which size you should knit.

The measurements given represent the dimensions of the knitting after finishing and blocking according to the pattern instructions and will help you identify which size you should knit. They can also be used to help make adjustments to the finished size of your knitting if needed. The Schematic and the measurements should be used to assist in the pinning-out process to ensure the finished piece is the correct size. Measurements are given in centimetres with inches shown in parentheses.

	1st Size	2nd Size	3rd Size	4th Size	5th Size	6th Size	7th Size	8th Size	9th Size	10th Size
To fit approx chest	71–76 (28–30)	81 (32)	86–91 (34–36)	97 (38)	102–107 (40–42)	112–117 (44–46)	122–127 (48–50)	132–137 (52–54)	142–147 (56–58)	152–157 (60–62)
Finished Measurements										
(a) Chest circumference	79½ (31¾)	88 (35¼)	96½ (38½)	105 (42)	114 (45½)	122½ (49)	131 (51¼)	139½ (55¾)	148 (59¼)	156½ (62½)
(b) Length to underarm (**Short Length**)	29 (11½)	29 (11½)	29 (11½)	29 (11½)	29 (11½)	29 (11½)	29 (11½)	29 (11½)	29 (11½)	29 (11½)
(b) Length to underarm (**Medium Length**)	40 (16)	40 (16)	40 (16)	40 (16)	40 (16)	40 (16)	40 (16)	40 (16)	40 (16)	40 (16)
(b) Length to underarm (**Long Length**)	50½ (20¼)	50½ (20¼)	50½ (20¼)	50½ (20¼)	50½ (20¼)	50½ (20¼)	50½ (20¼)	50½ (20¼)	50½ (20¼)	50½ (20¼)
(c) Armhole depth	18½ (7¼)	19½ (7¾)	19½ (7¾)	19½ (7¾)	22½ (9)	23 (9¼)	24 (9½)	24 (9½)	26 (10½)	27½ (11)
(d) Finished length (**Short Length**)	47½ (19)	48½ (19½)	48½ (19½)	48½ (19½)	51½ (20½)	52 (20¾)	53 (21¼)	53 (21¼)	55 (22)	56½ (22½)
(d) Finished length (**Medium Length**)	58½ (23½)	59½ (23¾)	59½ (23¾)	59½ (23¾)	62½ (25)	63 (25¼)	64 (25½)	64 (25½)	66 (26½)	67½ (27)
(d) Finished length (**Long Length**)	69 (27½)	70 (28)	70 (28)	70 (28)	73 (29¼)	73½ (29½)	74½ (29¾)	74½ (29¾)	76½ (30¾)	78 (31¼)
(e) Cross back	31 (12½)	31 (12½)	32½ (13)	33 (13¼)	34½ (13¾)	35½ (14¼)	36 (14½)	37 (14¾)	39 (15½)	41 (16½)
(g) Back neck width	14½ (5¾)	14½ (5¾)	15½ (6¼)	16 (6½)	17 (6¾)	17½ (7)	17½ (7)	18 (7¼)	19 (7½)	20½ (8¼)

SCHEMATIC

DIRECTIONS

BODY

Using smaller circular needle (80–100cm) and yarn B, cast on 217 (241, 265, 289, 313, 337, 361, 385, 409, 433) sts using long tail cast-on method. Join into a round, taking care not to twist sts, and place marker to indicate beginning of round.

Welt

Row 1 (RS): * K1, p1; rep from * to last st, k1.
Row 2 (WS): * K1, p1; rep from * to last st, k1.
These 2 rows form moss (seed) stitch pattern. Repeat these two rows until work measures 7½ (3in).

Lower Body

Change to larger circular needle (80–100cm).

Insert Steek

Set-up round (Inc): With RS facing, and using yarn A only, k to end of row, pm, then cast on 8 sts using backward loop method, placing a marker after first 4 cast-on sts to indicate new start of round; 8 steek sts cast-on.
Break yarn and rejoin at BOR marker.

Place Chart

Next round: Commencing with line 1 of Steek Chart A, work sts 5–8 once only, then commencing with line 1 of Lower Body Chart, work 12 st pattern repeat 18 (20, 22, 24, 26, 28, 30, 32, 34, 36) times across round, then work st 13 once only, then work sts 1–4 of Steek Chart A.
This round sets pattern. Continue in this manner until all 32 lines of Lower Body Chart and Steek Chart A have been completed. Depending on chosen length, repeat Chart A and Steek Chart A once (twice, thrice) more; on last round worked place side markers after 58 (64, 70, 76, 82, 88, 94, 100, 106, 112) sts from BOR marker, then place a second side marker after a further 109 (121, 133, 145, 157, 169, 181, 193, 205, 217) sts have been worked.
Your sts will now be divided as follows: 54 (60, 66, 72, 78, 84, 90, 96, 102, 108) sts for each front, 109 (121, 133, 145, 157, 169, 181, 193, 205, 217) sts for back, and 8 steek sts at centre front.

Armhole divide

Next round (Dec): Using Yarn A * k to 6 (6, 6, 6, 7, 7, 8, 8, 9, 10) sts beyond side marker, removing marker place last 12 (12, 12, 12, 14, 14, 16, 16, 18, 20) sts worked onto waste yarn, pm for armhole steek, then cast on 4 sts using backward loop method, pm; rep from * once more, k to end of round; 24 (24, 24, 24, 28, 28, 32, 32, 36, 40) sts placed on waste yarn, 8 steek sts cast-on, 209 (233, 257, 281, 301, 325, 345, 369, 389, 409) sts, including 16 steek sts.
Your sts will now be divided as follows: 48 (54, 60, 66, 71, 77, 82, 88, 93, 98) sts for each front, 2 sets of 4 steek sts for armholes, 97 (109, 121, 133, 143, 155, 165, 177, 187, 197) sts for back, and 8 steek sts at centre front.

UPPER BODY SHAPING

1st and 2nd sizes only
Armhole Shaping

Next round (Dec): Maintaining pattern as set and commencing with line 2 of correct Steek Chart B and Upper Body Chart for size being knitted, work sts 5–8 of Steek Chart B, * pattern to within 3 sts of armhole steek marker, k2tog, k1, sm, work sts 3–6 of Steek Chart B across next 4 sts, sm, k1, skp; rep from * once more, then pattern to last 4 sts, work sts 1–4 of Steek Chart B; 4 sts dec.
Maintaining pattern, continue as set decreasing 4 sts on each round a further 4 (10) times. A total of 20 (44) sts dec, 189 (189) sts.
Your sts will now be divided as follows: 43 (43) sts for each front, 2 sets of 4 steek sts for armholes, 87 (87) sts for back, and 8 steek sts at centre front.
Work in pattern for a further 7 (3) rounds without further shaping.

V-Neck Shaping

Next round (Dec): Maintaining pattern as set, work sts 5–8 of Steek Chart B, then pattern 1 st from Upper Body Chart, k2tog, pattern to last 7 sts, skp, pattern 1 st from Upper Body Chart, work sts 1–4 of Steek Chart B; 2 sts dec.
Next round: Maintaining pattern as set, work to end of round.
These two rounds set pattern. Continue as set, decreasing 2 sts on every other round a further 19 (19) times. A total of 40 (40) sts dec, 149 (149) sts. Your sts will now be divided as follows: 23 (23) sts for each front, 2 sets of 4 steek sts for armholes, 87 (87) sts for back, and 8 steek sts at centre front.

Continue without shaping until Upper Body Chart has been completed.

3rd, 4th, 5th, 6th, 7th, 8th, 9th and 10th sizes only

Armhole Shaping

Next round (Dec): Maintaining pattern as set and commencing with line 2 of correct Steek Chart B and Upper Body Chart for size being knitted, work sts 5–8 of Steek Chart B, * pattern to within 3 sts of armhole steek marker, k2tog, k1, sm, work sts 3–6 of Steek Chart B across next 4 sts, sm, k1, skp; rep from * once more, then pattern to last 4 sts, work sts 1–4 of Steek Chart B; 4 sts dec.
Maintaining pattern, continue as set decreasing 4 sts on each round a further 12 (11, 18, 18, 20, 18, 23, 23) times. A total of 52 (48, 76, 76, 84, 76, 96, 96) sts dec, 205 (233, 225, 249. 261, 293, 293, 313) sts.
Your sts will now be divided as follows: 47 (54, 52, 58, 61, 69, 69, 74) sts for each front, 2 sets of 4 steek sts for armholes, 95 (109, 105, 117, 123, 139, 139, 149) sts for back, and 8 steek sts at centre front.

Armhole and V-Neck Shaping

Next round (Dec): Maintaining pattern as set, work sts 5–8 of Steek Chart B, then pattern 1 st from Upper Body Chart, k2tog, * pattern to within 3 sts of armhole steek marker, k2tog, k1, sm, work sts 3–6 of Steek Chart B across next 4 sts, sm, k1, skp; rep from * once more, then pattern to last 7 sts, skp, pattern 1 st from Upper Body Chart, work sts 1–4 of Steek Chart B; 6 sts dec.
Next round (Dec): Maintaining pattern as set, * pattern to within 3 sts armhole steek marker, k2tog, k1, sm, work sts 3–6 of Steek Chart B across next 4 sts, sm, k1, skp; rep from * once more, then pattern to end of round; 4 sts dec.
These two rounds set pattern. Continue as set, decreasing 10 sts over two rounds a further 0 (3, 1, 3, 4, 8, 6, 7) times, then work the first round only – (–, –, once, once, –, once, once) more. A total of 10 (40, 20, 46, 56, 90, 76, 86) sts dec, 195 (193, 205, 203. 205, 203, 217, 227) sts.

Your sts will now be divided as follows: 44 (42, 46, 44, 44, 42, 46, 48) sts for each front, 2 sets of 4 steek sts for armholes, 91 (93, 97, 99, 101, 103, 109, 115) sts for back, and 8 steek sts at centre front.

V-Neck Shaping only

Next round (Dec): Maintaining pattern as set, work sts 5–8 of Steek Chart B, then pattern 1 st from Upper Body Chart, k2tog, pattern to last 7 sts, skp, pattern 1 st from Upper Body Chart, work sts 1–4 of Steek Chart B; 2 sts dec.
Next round: Maintaining pattern as set, work to end of round.
These two rounds set pattern. Continue as set, decreasing 2 sts on every other round a further 19 (17, 20, 18, 17, 15, 17, 18) times. A total of 40 (36, 42, 38, 36, 32, 36, 38) sts dec, 155 (157, 163, 165, 169, 171, 181, 189) sts.
Your sts will now be divided as follows: 24 (24, 25, 25, 26, 26, 28, 29) sts for each front, 2 sets of 4 steek sts for armholes, 91 (93, 97, 99, 101, 103, 109, 115) sts for back, and 8 steek sts at centre front.

Continue without shaping until Upper Body Chart has been completed.

Join Shoulders

1st, 5th, 6th, 7th, 8th, 9th and 10th sizes only

Next round: Using yarn A only, cast off 4 steek sts, * k to marker, remove marker, cast off 4 steek sts; rep from * twice more.
Divide front and back sts evenly over two needles. Using yarn A, graft 23 (25, 25, 26, 26, 28, 29) sts from left front to corresponding 23 (25, 25, 26, 26, 28, 29) sts on left back. Turn work and graft 23 (25, 25, 26, 26, 28, 29) sts from right front to corresponding 23 (25, 25, 26, 26, 28, 29) sts on right back. Leave remaining 41 (47, 49, 49, 51, 53, 57) sts for back neck on spare needle.

2nd, 3rd and 4th sizes only

Next round: Using yarn B only, cast off 4 steek sts, * k to marker, remove marker, cast off 4 steek sts; rep from * twice more.
Divide front and back sts evenly over two needles. Using yarn B, graft 23 (24, 24) sts from left front to corresponding 23 (24, 24) sts on left back. Turn work and graft 23 (24, 24) sts from right front to corresponding 23 (24, 24) sts on right back. Leave remaining 41 (43, 45) sts for back neck on spare needle.

All sizes
FRONT BAND
Reinforce and cut open front steek.

Short length only
Using smaller circular needle (100cm) and yarn B, and commencing at lower right front, pick up and k 95 (97, 99, 99, 105, 107, 109, 109, 115, 117) sts up right front, then k across 41 (41, 43, 45, 47, 49, 49, 51, 53, 57) sts on back neck, then pick up and k 95 (97, 99, 99, 105, 107, 109, 109, 115, 117) sts down left front; 231 (235, 241, 243, 257, 263, 267, 269, 283, 291) sts.

Medium length only
Using smaller circular needle (100cm) and yarn B, and commencing at lower right front, pick up and k 119 (121, 123, 123, 129, 131, 133, 133, 139, 141) sts up right front, then k across 41 (41, 43, 45, 47, 49, 49, 51, 53, 57) sts on back neck, then pick and k 119 (121, 123, 123, 129, 131, 133, 133, 139, 141) sts down left front; 279 (283, 289, 291, 305, 311, 315, 317, 331, 339) sts.

Long length only
Using smaller circular needle (100cm) and yarn B, and commencing at lower right front, pick up and k 143 (145, 147, 147, 153, 155, 157, 157, 163, 165) sts up right front, then k across 41 (41, 43, 45, 47, 49, 49, 51, 53, 57) sts on back neck, then pick and k 143 (145, 147, 147, 153, 155, 157, 157, 163, 165) sts down left front; 327 (331, 337, 339, 353, 359, 363, 365, 379, 387) sts.

All Lengths
Next row (WS): * k1, p1: rep from * to last st, k1.
Next row (RS): * k1, p1, rep from * to last st, k1.
This row sets moss (seed) stitch pattern. Repeat last 2 rows until band measures 2cm (¾in), ending with a RS row.
Cast off all sts.

ARM BANDS
Reinforce and cut open armhole steek.
Place 12 (12, 12, 12, 14, 14, 16, 16, 18, 20) sts held on waste yarn onto spare needle. Move first 6 (6, 6, 6, 7, 7, 8, 8, 9, 10) sts onto right needle tip of smaller circular needle (40–60cm) without knitting, and pm to indicate beginning of round. Join in yarn B and k across remaining 6 (6, 6, 6, 7, 7, 8, 8, 9, 10) sts held on spare needle, then pick up and k 42 (42, 44, 44, 50, 52, 54, 54, 58, 62) sts to shoulder, then pick up and k 42 (42, 44, 44, 50, 52, 54, 54, 58, 62) sts to underarm, k across remaining 6 (6, 6, 6, 7, 7, 8, 8, 9, 10) sts; 96 (96, 100, 100, 114, 118, 124, 124, 134, 144) sts.
Next round: * k1, p1; rep from * to end of round.
Next round: * p1, k1; rep from * to end of round.
These 2 rounds set moss (seed) stitch pattern. Continue until arm band measures 2cm (¾in). Cast off all sts.

FINISHING
Darn in all ends.
Soak in lukewarm soapy water and rinse if required. Pin out to size as shown on schematic and leave to dry flat.

Add press fastenings evenly spaced along straight front edges, placing lowest fastening 1cm (½in) from bottom edge and top fastening 1cm (½in) below commencement of front shaping. Stitch a button in place over each press fastening.

All Sizes

Lower Body Chart

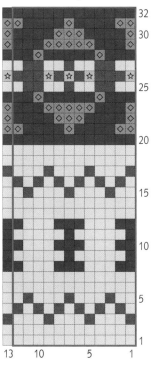

13   10   5   1

Steek Chart A

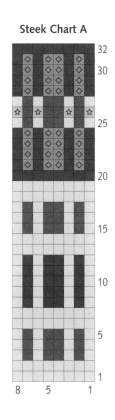

8   5   1

1st Size

Upper Body Chart

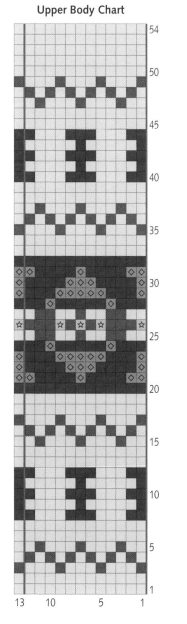

13   10   5   1

Steek Chart B

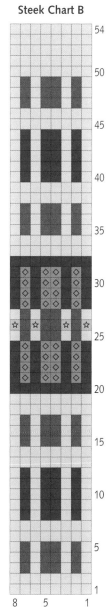

8   5   1

Key

▢	Yarn A (Dry Stone Wall)
▪	Yarn B (Undergrowth)
◇	Yarn C (Moss Covered Wall)
▪	Yarn D (Berry Picking)
☆	Yarn E (Hay Bale)
▢	Pattern repeat

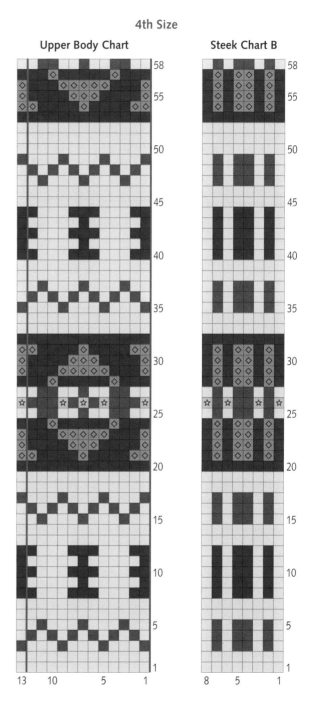

2nd & 3rd Sizes

Upper Body Chart

57
55
50
45
40
35
30
25
20
15
10
5
1

13   10   5   1

Steek Chart B

57
55
50
45
40
35
30
25
20
15
10
5
1

8   5   1

4th Size

Upper Body Chart

58
55
50
45
40
35
30
25
20
15
10
5
1

13   10   5   1

Steek Chart B

58
55
50
45
40
35
30
25
20
15
10
5
1

8   5   1

Key

- ☐ Yarn A (Dry Stone Wall)
- ■ Yarn B (Undergrowth)
- ◇ Yarn C (Moss Covered Wall)
- ■ Yarn D (Berry Picking)
- ☆ Yarn E (Hay Bale)
- ☐ Pattern repeat

5th Size

Upper Body Chart

Steek Chart B

6th Size

Upper Body Chart

Steek Chart B

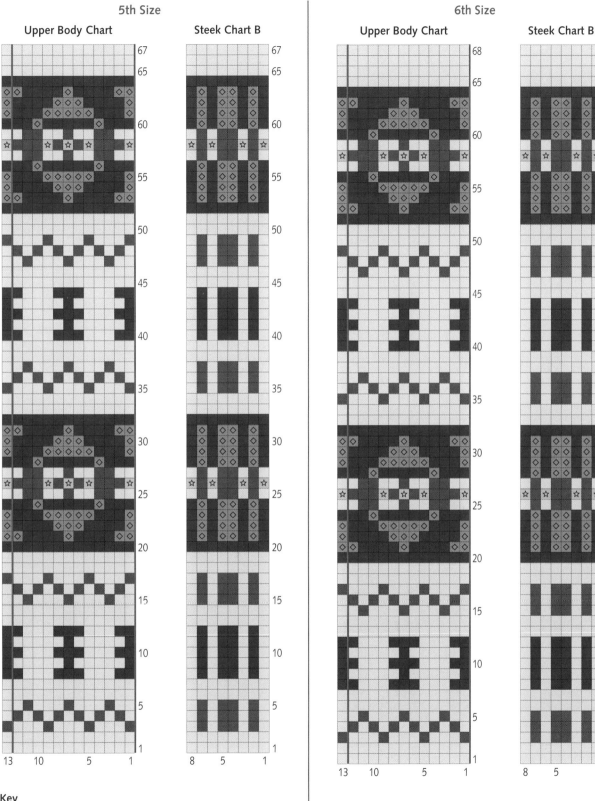

Key

▢	Yarn A (Dry Stone Wall)
■	Yarn B (Undergrowth)
◇	Yarn C (Moss Covered Wall)
■	Yarn D (Berry Picking)
☆	Yarn E (Hay Bale)
▢	Pattern repeat

7th & 8th Sizes

Upper Body Chart

Steek Chart B

9th Size

Upper Body Chart

Steek Chart B

Key

- ☐ Yarn A (Dry Stone Wall)
- ■ Yarn B (Undergrowth)
- ◇ Yarn C (Moss Covered Wall)
- ■ Yarn D (Berry Picking)
- ☆ Yarn E (Hay Bale)
- ☐ Pattern repeat

10th Size

Upper Body Chart   Steek Chart B

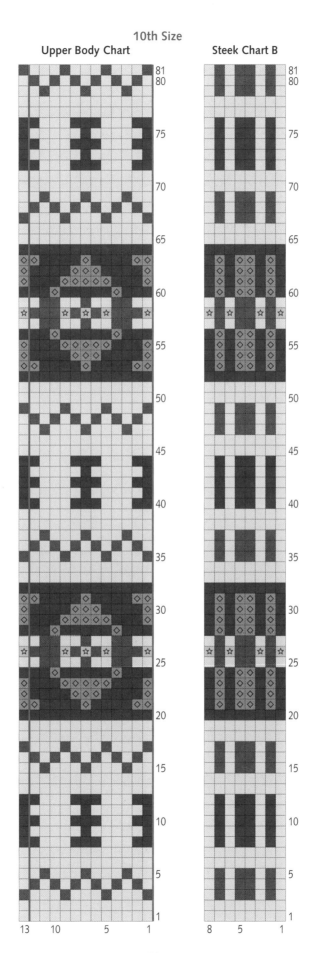

Key

⬜ Yarn A (Dry Stone Wall)

⬛ Yarn B (Undergrowth)

◇ Yarn C (Moss Covered Wall)

⬛ Yarn D (Berry Picking)

☆ Yarn E (Hay Bale)

⬜ Pattern repeat

Thank you to each and everyone of you who has bought a copy of
Evolution and has supported me through this strange and troubling year.

Thank you to Karen Butler, my Technical Editor and friend who has helped me keep
Evolution on track and to Helen and Gwenn, sample knitters extraordinaire who stepped in
when my aching shoulders meant I couldn't knit another stitch.

Most of all thank you to my husband Gavin and Charlie, my daughter, who between them enabled me to
bring my vision to life in the pages of this book. Charlie's sensitivity when photographing me put me at my ease. I
actually found myself enjoying the process and I think it shows in the stunning photographs she has taken. Gavin has
taken the raw material and turned it into the beautiful pages of this book, he has created the exquisite schematics and
of course, all the colourwork and lace charts in the patterns.

About the Author

Susan Crawford is a knitwear designer, author, publisher, yarn manufacturer and shepherdess who runs her own small business together with her husband Gavin form the their small family farm.

Susan runs an independent publishing company and writes knitting and fashion history books including A Stitch in Time, Vintage Knitting & Crochet Patterns volumes 1 and 2 and most recently The Vintage Shetland Project. Alongside her books and knitting patterns Susan has an ever-growing range of knitting yarns, specialising in British breed wools which she uses for all her design work. Alongside the ever popular Excelana and Fenella yarns, Susan has recently launched Barn and Byre both of which feature in Evolution and showcase Susan's new hand-dyed range of shades.

All of Susan's books, individual knitting and crochet patterns, yarn kits and of course, yarn, can pe purchased from our website – **www.susancrawfordvintage.com**

Keep in Touch
Sign up for Susan's regular newsletter via **www.susancrawfordvintage.com**

Join Susan on any of the following social media platforms:
Instagram: instagram.com/susancrawfordvintage   **Pinterest**: pinterest.co.uk/susancrawfordvintage
Twitter: twitter.com/astitchintime   **Ravelry**:   ravelry.com/groups/susancrawfordvintage
Facebook: facebook.com/susancrawfordvintage

You can now also join Susan's community on **Patreon**: www.patreon.com/susancrawford

We would love to see your finished projects from the book,
so if you are sharing on social media please use the hashtags
#susancrawfordvintage and **#evolutionknits**